Rufus M. Stanbrough

The Scriptural View of Divine Grace

Rufus M. Stanbrough

The Scriptural View of Divine Grace

ISBN/EAN: 9783337780180

Printed in Europe, USA, Canada, Australia, Japan

Cover: Foto ©Lupo / pixelio.de

More available books at **www.hansebooks.com**

THE
SCRIPTURAL VIEW

—OF—

DIVINE GRACE:

Is it Unversalist, Arminian or Calvinistic?

TEN PROPOSITIONS.

BY

RUFUS M. STANBROUGH.

:: Fleming H. Revell ::

CHICAGO: | NEW YORK:
148 and 150 Madison Street. | 12 Bible House, Astor Place.

• :: Publisher of Evangelical Literature :: •

PREFACE.

Cheerful acknowledgment is hereby made of help received from the published works of Prof. Charles Hodge, D. D., President Jonathan Edwards, D. D., Rev. James B. Walker and others.

In the interpretation of a book so large as the Bible, and which deals with such momentous themes, it is probably to be expected that there will not be complete unanimity.

The author's preference among evangelical systems, with reasons therefor, is indicated under Proposition VII, in discussing Rom. v : 18, 19; I Cor. xv : 22, and Eph. i : 10. As a help to the right understanding of one momentous Bible theme—man's destiny under Divine dealing—this little book is sent forth like a ship on the wide ocean. May the blessing of the God of Truth accompany it, and make it an aid to the victory of Truth throughout all this happy American land.

WEST HURLEY, N. Y., *Nov.* 1, 1889.

CONTENTS.

PROPOSITIONS: (Abbreviated).   PAGE.

I. The Christ is the Judge of all mankind 8

II. The judgment is distinct from that at Jerusalem ... 10

III. The results of judgment are experienced after physical death 29

IV. In the judgment the Christ will be personally visible.. 55

V. Before the judgment the deceased Saints will experience a bodily resurrection; and living Christians a bodily transformation 67

VI. Before the judgment the wicked dead will experience a bodily resurrection 83

VII. The wicked will be condemned in the judgment which follows their bodily resurrection; and will never be restored to the favor of God 102

VIII. Methods of Scriptural interpretation used by our doctrinal opponents are wrong; since those methods teach contradictory doctrines 259

IX. The teachings of Nature do not favor the idea that mankind universally will attain unto holiness and happiness. 264

X. Endless punishment of the impenitent wicked does not prove that God is unjust 277

THE SCRIPTURAL VIEW OF DIVINE GRACE.

Introductory.

The subject that is now to be investigated, is one of vast importance to every human being. No one so lofty, no one so lowly as to remain unaffected, either in this present life or in the life beyond the grave, by the views which he cherishes respecting this vital matter.

As opinions which a pilot holds concerning the currents and counter currents which his ship is to meet, influence him to a specific mode of guiding the vessel and securing its safety, so the beliefs which possess the human soul exercise a powerful influence in determining the course which it shall choose among the breakers and the billows of the broad sea of life. If that sea be never swept by angry storms; if that sea be never white with wrathful waves; if that sea never inclose with arms of death the deceived voyager who has trusted to its apparent calmness, then let the traveler upon it drink deep of the cup of fate, and take no thought of the perils of the morrow. But if its waves still toss the broken fragments of the wreck, and on its air there still is borne to the listening ear the sad wail of the sinking, let him who is still to voyage on its treacherous surface, take some heed that his vessel be stanch—his pilot wise—his voyage safe and blessed. That there is need of forethought, that there is need of action, it is the purpose of these remarks to show.

They will take the form of propositions, each one of which we shall endeavor by solid proof to sustain.

Proposition I. The Scriptures teach that Jesus Christ has been appointed of God the Judge of the entire race of man.

This truth Christ taught. He says in John v : 22, 23, 27, " The Father judgeth no man, but hath committed all judgment unto the Son; that all men should honor the Son even as they honor the Father. * * And hath given him authority to execute judgment also because he is the Son of man."

This truth the apostles taught: Phil. ii: 9,

10, 11, "God hath also highly exalted him and given him a name which is above every name; that at the name of Jesus every knee should bow, of things in heaven, and things in earth, and things under the earth; and that every tongue should confess that Jesus Christ is Lord, to the glory of God the Father."

This passage teaches that Christ's power as Judge extends also over the dead: for it is plain that in this life all knees do not bow at the name of Jesus, and all tongues do not confess that Jesus Christ is Lord; therefore this bowing and confession must take place after death. Christ is Judge of the dead as well as of the living.

This power of judgment is not limited to the Jews, but extends over all nations. Paul taught a future judgment to the men of Athens, Acts xvii: 30, 31. "God now commandeth all men everywhere, to repent, because he hath appointed a day in the which he will judge the world in righteousness by that man whom he hath ordained; whereof he hath given assurance unto all men, in that he hath raised him from the dead."

This judgment will be as universal as the command to repent. And the command to repent reaches every sinner who hears of the gospel of Christ.

Luke xxiv:47: "And that repentance and remission of sins should be preached in his name among all nations, beginning at Jerusalem." This judgment is so universal as to include even those sinners who have been destitute of a written revelation, Rom. ii:11, 12, 16: "For there is no respect of persons with God. For as many as have sinned without law, shall also perish without law: and as many as have sinned in the law, shall be judged by the law, * * in the day when God shall judge the secrets of men by Jesus Christ."

Proposition II. The Scriptures teach a coming of Christ to judgment distinct from his coming at the destruction of Jerusalem.

The truth of this proposition is very evident from the fact that the unbelieving Gentiles were not judged at the destruction of Jerusalem.

Jerusalem was destroyed A. D. 70, but years before this the gospel of Christ had been preached at Rome and Corinth, at Galatia and Ephesus, at Thessalonica, Phillippi, Athens and elsewhere. And while there were many believers, there were still great multitudes who remained impenitent and unbelieving. For thirty-five years previous to the city's destruction, the faithful embassadors of Jesus had been preaching to the nations; and surely no one will affirm that all those throughout the nations who rejected the gospel of Christ, were *gathered* together at Jerusalem and *punished*. And if they were not so gathered, then is there another coming of Christ than his coming at Jerusalem; for the Scriptures clearly teach that the unbelieving of the Gentiles are to be judged.

The epistle to the Romans was written before the destruction of Jerusalem, and in the 2d chap. vs. 5–9 is as follows: "But after thy hardness and impenitent heart treasurest up unto thyself wrath against the day of wrath and revelation of the righteous judgment of God; who will render to every man according to his deeds: to them who by patient continuance in well doing, seek for glory and honor, and immortality, eternal life: but unto them that are contentious and do not obey the truth, but obey unrighteousness, indignation and wrath, tribulation and anguish, upon every soul of man that doeth evil; of the Jew first, and also of the Gentile."

Now as these unbelieving Gentiles must be

judged, and were not judged at the destruction of Jerusalem, it follows that there must be another coming of Christ to judgment distinct from his coming at the fall of Jerusalem.

To the Athenians also, Paul said, "He will judge the world in righteousness, by that man whom he hath ordained." (Acts xvii : 31).

We are taught also, that Felix, the Roman governor, *trembled* as Paul "reasoned of righteousness, temperance and judgment to come," (Acts xxiv : 25). Surely the destruction of Jerusalem would not make a Roman governor tremble, when the destruction was to be wrought by the Romans themselves.

The truth of this proposition is also evident from the fact that the believing Gentiles were not judged at the fall of the doomed city. Many had already sealed with their life's blood the purity of their faith, and the strength of their love; and their souls had passed to glory. They were not judged at the fall of the city.

Nor were the churches of the believers at Corinth, Phillippi, Rome and Thessalonica, Galatia, Ephesus, and Colosse, judged at the fall of the city. Therefore there is another coming of Christ to judgment; and one distinct from his coming at the destruction of Jerusalem.

Very decisive testimony against confining to the destruction of Jerusalem the coming of Christ to judgment, is contained in Matt. xxiv: 29–31, together with Mark xiii: 27, and Luke xxi: 35.

Respecting these passages, two things are to be noticed. The first is, that special events are predicted to occur at or before the coming of the Son of man which did not occur at or before the destruction of Jerusalem. Matt. xxiv: 31 is, "And he shall send his angels with a great sound of a trumpet, and they shall gather his elect from the four winds, from one end of heaven to the other." Now at the destruction of Jerusalem there was no gathering of believers "from one end of heaven to the other." If so, where is the proof? None is to be found in sacred or profane history. The Christians in Judea and especially Jerusalem, fled into the mountains, and some of them went into the little village of Pella; but surely this does not fulfil the broad statement "from one end of heaven to the other." The parallel, Mark xiii: 27 is "And then shall he send his angels, and shall gather together his elect from the four winds, from the uttermost part of earth to the uttermost part of heaven." Here Christ plainly unites heaven with earth as a place from which the angels shall gather his elect. Now this does not at all suit the theory that the coming referred to took place at Jerusalem's destruction. But it does suit perfectly the idea that reference is had to a coming of Christ to judgment subsequent to that at Jerusalem and still future. For, at the still future coming to judgment, " the dead in Christ shall rise first, then we which are alive and remain, shall be caught up together with them ; " and " Abraham and Isaac and Jacob and all the prophets" and those "from the east and west, and from the north and south, shall sit down in the kingdom of God," while the wicked contemporaries of Christ shall be excluded. (I Thess. iv : 16, 17), (Luke xiii : 28, 29).

They shall be gathered from the end of earth to the end of heaven. This of course, did not take place before nor at the fall of Jerusalem.

Luke xxi : 35 is, " For as a snare shall it come on all them that dwell on the face of the whole earth." It is not true that Christ's coming in providence, at the destruction of Jerusalem, came as a snare " on all them that dwell on the face of the whole earth." It did not come as a snare to the Parthians, the Britons, the Celts, the Arabians, the Chinese, nor the Africans. And doubtless, owing to the small facilities for communicating information, some of the distant tribes of the earth knew nothing of the conflict between the Roman and the Jew. And therefore that coming of Christ in providence, could not come on them as a snare.

The only nation on which the destruction of Jerusalem can be properly said to have come as a snare, is the Jewish nation. It did not come on the Romans as a snare. They planned it; they fought for it; they rejoiced at its accomplishment. Nor on the neutral nations; but alone on the Jews. This, indeed, our doctrinal opponents seem to admit. Referring to the destruction of Jerusalem, Rev. I. D. Williamson, D. D. (*Defence of Univ.; p.* 123), speaks of " the Gentiles entering into that knowledge of God which is declared to be 'life eternal,' and the Jews going away into a state of perpetual chastisement, until the fulness of the Gentiles be come in."

Now it is surely improper to affirm both that because of the destruction of Jerusalem the Gentiles entered into " life eternal," and also that the same destruction of Jerusalem came on the Gentiles as a snare. The entering into life eternal, is something desirable; the coming of that day as a snare, is, in the mind of Christ, something to be shunned.

But if the destruction of Jerusalem came not on the Gentiles as a snare, then is there yet to be a coming of Christ which shall come as a snare "on all them that dwell on the face of the whole earth."

And yet further, since that day is to come as a snare "on all them that dwell on the face of the whole earth," therefore the command of Christ, "Watch ye therefore, and pray always that ye may be accounted worthy to escape all these things that shall come to pass, and to stand before the Son of man," is given to Christians "on the face of the whole earth." But what need was there for a Christian in China or Britain, or for the Ethiopian baptized by Philip, to watch and pray always lest he should experience suffering at the destruction of Jerusalem? All the case demanded was to keep away from the devoted city. And that the great multitude of Christians would have done, had there been no revealed warning given. Christ certainly meant more by his "watch and pray always" than "keep away from Jerusalem."

And respecting these passages, the second thing to be noticed is, that even if the special events predicted to occur at or before the coming of the Son of man did occur at or before the destruction of Jerusalem, yet still was there predicted to occur a coming of the Son of man subsequent to the destruction of the city, and which coming was to be attended or preceded by the same special events; namely, the gathering of the elect from the end of earth to the end of heaven; and the (day) coming as a snare on the face of all them that dwell on the face of the whole earth; and the mourning of all the tribes of the earth.

The prediction reads thus (Matt. xxiv : 29 —31), "Immediately after the tribulation of those days, shall the sun be darkened, and the moon shall not give her light, and the stars shall fall from heaven, and the powers of the heavens shall be shaken. And then shall appear the sign of the Son of man in heaven; and then shall all the tribes of the earth mourn, and they shall see the Son of man coming in the clouds of heaven with power and great glory. And he shall send his angels with a great sound of a trumpet, and they shall gather together his elect from the four winds, from one end of heaven to the other."

Notice that *after* the tribulation of those days, occurs *first*, the darkening of sun and moon—the falling of the stars—and the shaking of the powers of heaven.

Notice that *after* the tribulation of those days, occurs *second*, the appearing of the sign of the Son of man in heaven.

Notice that *after* the tribulation of those days, occurs *third*, the mourning of all the tribes of the earth, their seeing the Son of man coming with power and great glory in the clouds of heaven, and the gathering by the angels, of the elect from one end of heaven to the other.

Now since beyond all possibility of honest mistake by ordinary intelligence, this seeing the Son of man coming in the clouds of heaven is placed *after* the tribulation of those days, it becomes very important to ascertain what is meant by "the tribulation of those days."

And beyond all possibility of honest and intelligent doubt, the tribulation of those days was when the Roman armies were menacing and destroying the Jewish city. For Christ says (Matt. xxiv: 15, 16, 19 – 22), "When ye therefore shall see the abomination of desolation spoken of by Daniel the prophet stand in the holy place, then let them which be in Judea flee into the mountains. * * And wo unto them that are with child, and to them that give suck in those days. But pray ye that your flight be not in the winter, neither on the Sabbath day. For then shall be great tribulation such as was not since the beginning of the world to this time, no, nor ever shall be. And except those days should be shortened there should no flesh be saved; but for the elect's sake those days shall be shortened." Clearly then the time of "the tribulation of those days" is the time when the Roman armies were gathering and were gathered about the Jewish city; that is, the time of Jerusalem's destruction.

Now with this coming of the Son of man, thus clearly subsequent to the fall of Jerusalem, is connected the mourning of all the tribes of the earth, and the gathering of the elect from one end of heaven to the other. And therefore, even if it could be proved that there was a species of fulfilment of the events connected with the coming of the Son of man now being considered, at the destruction of Jerusalem, it could only be a typical, a foreshadowing fulfillment of that subsequent and grander coming when "all the tribes of the earth shall mourn, and they shall see the Son of man coming in the clouds of heaven with power and great glory."

As an objection to this interpretation, which asserts a special coming of Christ to judgment subsequent to the destruction of

Jerusalem, the words of Christ in Matt. xxiv: 34, have been presented, " Verily I say unto you, this generation shall not pass away till all these things be fulfilled."

Those who present this objection would restrict the duration of "this generation" to the duration of the lives of Christ's contemporaries—to one link in the series of the human race.

This necessarily forbids a prediction by the previous passages, of a coming of Christ to special judgment subsequent to the fall of Jerusalem, unless the coming at Jerusalem, while actual, might also be typical, and not complete and final. Then Christ says, This one of the series of generations, shall not pass away till my coming at Jerusalem's destruction shall be actually fulfilled, and my coming subsequent to that be typically fulfilled. This principle of typical interpretation is really applicable to prophecies of Scripture, or both Universalist and Orthodox have erred in the same manner in the interpretation of the prophecies of Daniel. For both have referred the "abomination of desolation" spoken of by that prophet to Antiochus Epiphanes, the fierce persecutor of the Jews; yet Christ undoubtedly refers that same abomination of desolation to events occurring in close connection with a then future fall of Jerusalem. And by this same principle so eminent a theologian as Olshausen explains Matt. xxiv: 34. His words are "View the prophecy with reference to the immediate present, but in such a manner, that everything includes a further reference to the future." That there *must* be this reference to the future if "this generation" means only the earth-life of Christ's contemporaries, is clearly shown by the indisputable fact that the coming of Christ spoken of, occurs *after* the destruction of Jerusalem. But there is no necessity whatever for limiting the duration of "this generation" to that of a single link in the human series.

The classical meaning of the original word (genea) as given in Greek lexicons is birth, race, generation, family. In the following quotations from Homer wherever the word *race* occurs, it is the translation of the word in question, (genea):

Od. 16, 117. "For thus hath the son of Saturn made our *race* single ; Arcesius begot an only son, Laertes, his father again begot Ulysses alone ; but Ulysses having begot me alone, left me in the palace."

Od. 20, 193. "What stranger is this, O swineherd, that has lately come to our house?

from what men does he boast himself to be? where are his *race* and paternal country?"

Od. 15, 175. "As this (eagle) coming from the mountains, where is its *race* and birth, snatched away the goose which had been nurtured delicately in the house; so Ulysses" etc., etc.

Il. 6, 211. In reply to a question respecting his race, Glaucus, after mentioning the names of his paternal ancestors for five generations, says, "From this *race* and blood do I boast myself to be."

Il. 10, 68. Agamemnon directing Menelaus, says, "Shout aloud whithersoever thou goest, and enjoin them to be watchful, accosting each man by a name from his paternal *race*, honorably addressing all."

Il. 5, 265. Speaking of the horses of Æneas, Diomede says, "They are of that *breed* which far-seeing Jove gave as a price to Taos for his son Ganymede; wherefore they are the best of steeds." In this last quotation, *breed* is a translation of the word in question (genea). Respecting the accuracy of the translation of the word in these quotations, no question can be successfully raised. Not only are the quotations from the literal and standard translations of T. A. Buckley, but the connection in which the word stands, also evidences the accuracy of its translation. In the Septuagint the word (genea) is used to translate the Hebrew mishpachah, which means a family, a nation, as in Lev. xxv : 41, Jer. viii:3 ; and also hăm, which means a people, a nation, as in Lev. xx : 18.

In the New Testament Christ himself, in Luke xvi:8, uses the word in a sense which requires a length of time equal to the duration of a race; and which sense is equivalent to that of *kind* or *race*. He says, " The children of this world are wiser in their generation (genea) than the children of light." Here Christ affirms or implies that the children of this world have a "generation," and also that the children of light have a "generation." And the word is in the singular number. Now the generation of the children of this world endures as long as the children of this world endure. And also the generation of the children of light endures as long as the children of light endure. The generation of each class has endured until the nineteenth century, and will endure until Christ's future and visible coming. And now so far from being compelled in our translation of "generation" (genea) as occurring in Matt. xxiv:34 to limit its meaning to that of a single link in the human series, we have in addition two plain, honest meanings from which to choose. With light from the classics and the Septuagint we may interpret the word as meaning race, people, family, nation; and understand Christ as referring it to the Jewish nation; or with Christ himself in Luke xvi:8 attaching to the word a moral idea we may understand Him to refer to His believing followers, to the race—the family of Christians. Christ certainly sometimes spake with a meaning which was hidden from careless hearers. When He said, "Destroy this temple and in three days I will raise it up," He was understood to mean the Jewish temple, but an unquestionable authority informs us that "He spake of the temple of His body." And just as in the one case Christ spoke of a really spiritual temple, so in the other case He may have spoken of a spiritual generation.

So far as Christ's still future coming to a special judgment of the nations is concerned, it is immaterial whether he be understood to refer to the Jewish race or to Christians. But so long as in the classics, the Septuagint, and the New Testament, the word has a meaning extending beyond that of a single link in the human chain, it is most certainly unreasonable to affirm that in Matt. xxiv:34, when there is nothing in the context to demand it, the word in question *must* be interpreted to mean but a single link in the series. And therefore, when Christ says, "This generation (genea) shall not pass away till all these things be fulfilled," He presents no argument whatever against His coming to a special judgment of the nations subsequent to the destruction of Jerusalem.

Now let us notice a statement of Christ in Luke xxi:24: "And Jerusalem shall be trodden down of the Gentiles until the times of the Gentiles be fulfilled."

Now, beyond all question, the times of the Gentiles have not yet been fulfilled. And the same principle of strict interpretation by which our doctrinal opponents (though in vain) would confine the time of the events to the duration of a single generation, binds them to include in the "all things" to be fulfilled the duration of time which is used in fulfilling "the times of the Gentiles." "Jerusalem shall be trodden down of the Gentiles *until* the times of the Gentiles be *fulfilled*." Now since this length of time is one of the things, and is therefore included in the "all things" to be fulfilled, and since "the times of the Gentiles are not yet fulfilled, "it follows of necessity that the prediction of Christ is untrue. To such a deplorable issue does that interpretation conduct which would confine the "this generation" in question to a single link in the human series.

It is a correct and well understood principle of interpretation that a particular word or phrase in any sentence means not what that word or phrase means when used in other connections, but what it means in the connection in which it stands. When a venerable President at Yale or Princeton addresses a perhaps wayward youth as, "My son," etc., he is, of course, not to be understood as referring to a blood relationship, simply because he uses the words "my son." And yet these words as generally used do express that relationship. When a Catholic refers to his parish priest as "father," he is, of course, not to be understood as referring to a blood relationship simply because he uses the word "father." And yet that word as generally used does express that relationship. In the cases specified, though the words "my son" and "father" are not used in their primary but in a derived meaning, yet is that derived meaning perfectly legitimate. The meaning of the words is determined by the connection in which they stand. Another correct and well understood principle of interpretation is, that when a person of admitted intelligence and truthfulness uses a word of two meanings, and the word in one meaning conflicts with his intelligence or truthfulness, and in the other meaning does not thus conflict, it *must* be understood in that meaning which harmonizes with his intelligence and truthfulness.

Now put together these facts:

The word in question has different meanings. The intelligence and truthfulness of Christ no Christian denies.

The prediction undeniably includes at least a single particular which has not yet been fulfilled.

The understanding of the word in one of its meanings conflicts with the intelligence or truthfulness of Christ.

The understanding of the word in another of its meanings, harmonizes with the intelligence and truthfulness of Christ. And now in view of these facts when the question arises what meaning, shall we attribute to "generation" (genea) in Matt. xxiv:34, will any believer in Christianity hesitate to answer —the word in question *must* have that meaning attributed to it which harmonizes with the intelligence and truthfulness of Christ. And that meaning is, not a single link in the human series, but a race, a people, a family.

And now in closing our remarks on "this generation" we may state that there is no impropriety in supposing that Christ may have with wise and benevolent design, employed a word which means either a single generation or a race. His purpose in the prediction was to make his followers watchful and prayerful. And the very fact that the word is applicable to different lengths of time is adapted to promote the accomplishment of that purpose. Had it meant only a single generation it would for all time subsequent to that generation have tended to diminish faith and zeal. Had it meant only a race, it might have tended to slacken the watchfulness and prayer of all primitive Christians who did not believe in the speedy extinction of the Jewish or Christian people.

Neither God nor Christ revealed to the disciples all truth whatsoever, but that which was for their good. Christ himself tells them, "But of that day and hour knoweth no man, no, not the angels of heaven, but my Father only." Now this very uncertainty of the time, as any one may see, is adapted to quicken effort in all generations except that nearest to the fulfilment of the coming. And thus to stimulate successive generations we may reasonably conclude that Christ designedly used a word capable of indicating different lengths of time.

Proposition III. The Scriptures teach a coming of Christ to judgment not only distinct from his coming at the destruction of Jerusalem, but also distinct from his coming in the judgments of the present earthly life; a judgment, the results of which are experienced after physical death.

This is true of believers and unbelievers. First, of believers:

Paul teaches this in II Tim. iv:6-8. He says: "I am now ready to be offered, and the time of my departure is at hand. I have fought a good fight, I have finished my course. I have kept the faith; henceforth there is laid up for me a crown of righteousness which the Lord, the righteous Judge shall give me at that day; and not to me only, but unto all them also that love his appearing."

Paul is now near to death—and near to death for Jesus' sake. He considered his course as finished, and he tells Timothy and us that henceforth there is " laid up," reserved, kept safe, not now given, but "laid up" for him a crown of righteousness. And this crown of righteousness was to be given at a future day; "which the righteous Judge *shall* give me at that day." Plainly at a day subsequent to his own death. And plainly also, Paul considers that there is a connection between his conduct in the earthly life and his receiving, in the life beyond the grave, the crown of righteousness. He mentions his good conduct. He fought well, he kept the faith, he was to die for Jesus' sake; after that there was laid up a reward which he would receive at a subsequent day.

This reward was also to be given by a righteous judge. Now a righteous judge is one who judges righteously; not one who is indifferent to right and wrong, but one who approves the right, and condemns the wrong. Therefore, Paul's crown of righteousness, to be received from the righteous Judge, is given in consequence of his righteous conduct, which the judge approves and rewards.

Where in all God's revelations is there language like this? "I have been a blasphemer and a persecutor. I am still impenitent and wicked and am about to die, hating man and unreconciled to God; henceforth there is laid up for me a crown of righteousness which the Lord, the righteous Judge, shall give me at that day." Does it not shock every sentiment of the Christian heart?

Yet just this is the teaching of those who deny a connection between faith and holiness in this life, and the reward of blessedness in the life to come.

"He that justifieth the wicked, and he that condemneth the just, even they both are abomination to the Lord." (Prov. xvii:15.)

Let us look at Scripture testimony in the case of another eminent man, Moses, the Jewish lawgiver. We find it in Heb. xi:24-27. "By faith Moses, when he was come to years, refused to be called the son of Pharaoh's daughter; choosing rather to suffer affliction with the people of God, than to enjoy the pleasures of sin for a season; esteeming the reproach of Christ greater riches than the treasures in Egypt; for he had respect unto the recompense of reward."

Affliction with the people of God rather than the pleasures of sin for a season. His good choice and work lasting through life, and evidently not receiving the reward on earth. The same with his esteeming the reproach of Christ greater riches than the treasures in Egypt. His recompense of reward was beyond the grave. He died even before entering the land of promise. Something of that recompense of reward we learn in the Gospels. Luke ix:28–31. "Jesus took Peter and John and James, and went up into a mountain to pray. And as he prayed the fashion of his countenance was altered, and his raiment was white and glistering. And behold there talked with him two men which were Moses and Elias; who appeared in glory, and spake of his decease which he should accomplish at Jerusalem." This was a part of that recompense of reward unto which Moses had respect.

Among the instances of believers, let us take Christ himself. Phil. ii:7–9. "Christ Jesus made himself of no reputation, and took upon himself the form of a servant, and was made in the likeness of men; and being found in fashion as a man, he humbled himself, and became obedient unto death, even the death of the cross, *Wherefore* God also hath highly exalted him, and given him a name which is above every name." That is on account of Christ's voluntary humiliation and death, and *after* his death God highly exalted him. And furthermore, Christ is commended unto believers as an example in this very particular of future reward.

Heb. xii:1, 2. "Let us run with patience

the race that is set before us, looking unto Jesus the author and finisher of faith; who *for the joy that was set before him endured the cross*, despising the shame, and is set down at the right hand of the throne of God."

Here we have the assertion that Jesus "for the joy that was set before him, endured the cross." Now Jesus endured the cross until the last moment of his life; and the enduring of the cross was a means to an end; consequently the means must be used before the gaining of the end, and therefore the end which was " the joy set before him " was not gained until life was extinct.

And plainly as language can teach it, we are taught a connection between the conduct of Jesus in the life on earth, and the reward of Jesus in the life subsequent to bodily death. How can the force of this plain teaching be avoided? The only possible method is to affirm that in this particular Jesus differed from other men. We ask for the Scriptural proof. Those who would make such an affirmation deny the Saviour's divinity and affirm him to be a mere man. If a mere man, then other mere men hold the same relation to the laws of God as he. And if there be in Jesus' case a connection between conduct on earth and reward in the future world, then most certainly the same connection holds in the case of other men.

In Heb. xi:35, is also taught a connection between conduct in this life and reward in the next.

"Women received their dead raised to life. Others were tortured not accepting deliverance, that they might obtain a better resurrection."

There are different resurrections—national, reputational, moral, universal, or such as all mankind *must* experience subsequent to bodily death, and the resurrection unto the glories and bliss of the future life, which all believers are to experience.

Which of these different resurrections does the apostle mean by the "better resurrection"?

Not national, for he is not speaking of nations but of individuals; not reputational, for these ancient heroes *all* lived by faith and Moses among them "esteemed the *reproach* of Christ greater riches than the *treasures* of Egypt."

Not *moral*, for those who were tortured not accepting deliverance, were *believers*, and already possessed the moral resurrection.

Not the universal resurrection which all mankind must experience subsequent to bodily death; for if *all must* experience *that* independent of moral conduct, what need of undergoing torture (even unto death) to obtain it?

And we are shut up to the conclusion that by the "better resurrection" the apostle means the resurrection of the faithful unto the glories and bliss of the future world, a "better resurrection" from which the unfaithful and wicked are excluded.

Having now advanced Scriptural proof abundantly sufficient to convince any impartial mind that there is a connection between the conduct of believers in this life and their condition beyond the grave, we proceed to show that the same connection exists in the case of the unbelieving and the wicked.

This truth Christ teaches in Luke xii:4, 5: "And I say unto you my friends, be not afraid of them that kill the body, and after that have no more that they can do. But I will forewarn you whom ye shall fear. Fear him, which *after he hath killed* hath power to cast into hell; yea, I say unto you, Fear him."

Christ teaches mankind here that there is a being who after he hath killed has power to cast into hell. And that they should fear this being more than they fear them who can do nothing more, cause no more suffering, after they have killed the body.

Now it is trifling to affirm that, though the being spoken of possesses the power to cast the soul into hell, yet he will never, he can never, exercise that power. The ability to exercise that power is the very basis of the warning. If he under all circumstances, never can or never will exercise the power, the warning loses all its force. Who fears a cannon that never shoots—a sword that never smites, a law that never punishes? Had these friends of Christ to whom the warning was given understood that the power of casting into hell would never or could never be exercised, the warning might just as well have never been spoken. And really it would have been no warning, but a simple statement of the possession of the power.

A warning always implies, if no precaution is taken, a danger of the occurrence of that event against which the warning is given. And if moral obligation, or any cause whatever, perpetually prevent the exercise of the power of casting into hell after death, then the warning of Christ is no warning at all. But as He calls it a warning, and as He is a teacher of truth and not of error, therefore, if the warning be not heeded, the event against which the warning is given will assuredly happen.

This truth Christ teaches also in Matt. xxvi:24: "The Son of man goeth as it is written of him: but wo unto that man by whom the Son of man is betrayed! It had been good for that man if he had not been born."

The woe pronounced upon Judas was because of his betrayal of Jesus. After the commission of that great crime he experienced remorse of conscience, gave back the price of his wickedness, and went and hanged himself. These events can by no means fulfil the terribleness of that saying: "It had been good for that man if he had not been born." They were all experienced probably in less than twenty-four hours after the betrayal. The betrayal occurred at night—the condemnation the next day. And "then Judas, when he saw that He was condemned, repented himself, and brought again the thirty pieces of silver to the chief priests and elders, * * * and cast down the pieces of silver in the temple, and went and hanged himself." (Matt. xxvii:3, 5.)

Surely, if all the woe of Judas was experienced in the brief space of time between the betrayal and the hanging; and if, after death, his soul, or soul and body united, enjoy a bliss that is everlasting, then the words of Jesus teach not truth but error. To make these words truthful it is absolutely necessary that, the whole existence of Judas Iscariot considered, his misery exceed his happiness. This certainly carries the misery of Judas into, and a long way into, the world that is eternal.

On this passage Olshausen remarks: "The form of execration (kalon een auto, etc.,) is an expression signifying the deepest apostacy, and utter perdition. It is so strong that it intimates the exclusion of every hope. For although eternal life is to be won afterward, yet must the mere fact of being born be a benefit."

Krummacher says: "This inscription placed over the grave of his unhappy disciple by the Lord himself is the most fearful and affrighting utterance of the whole Bible." And when we remember that Jesus said, Let your communication be Yea, yea; Nay, nay: for whatsoever is more than these cometh of evil, it gives increased force to the conviction that Jesus then taught a strict literal truth.

The fact also that our Lord terms Judas "the son of perdition," and affirms that he is lost (John xvii:12), teaches that there is condemnation in the future world,

The teaching of Jesus in regard to persons who die in their sins, clearly proves a state of condemnation beyond the grave. In John viii:21 he says, "I go my way, and ye shall seek me, and shall die in your sins: whither I go ye cannot come."

After their death in sin they could not go where Jesus had gone. Now, Christ represents himself as going after death unto the heavenly Father, saying in John xvii:11: "And now I am no more in the world, but these (disciples) are in the world, and I come to thee." And to the thief upon the cross he also said: "To-day shalt thou be with me in paradise." (Luke xxiii:43.)

These statements leave no doubt as to where Jesus went at death. Christ went to the heavenly Father; where did they go to whom he said: "Whither I go ye cannot come." Christ also said of these: "Ye are of your father the devil, and the lusts of your father ye will do." Now if they were children of the devil and were to die "in their sins" we are shut up to the belief that they would not at death enter heaven, the moral character of whose inhabitants is so different from theirs; "for whither I go ye cannot come," and "without holiness no man shall see the Lord." Now, if they did not enter heaven, they must, since souls are conscious after bodily death, have entered some place inferior to heaven—a place doubtless of condemnation and punishment.

Let us now examine some of the teachings of the apostles of Christ.

In 1 Cor. ix:26, 27, Paul states of himself, "So fight I not as one that beateth the air; but I keep under my body and bring it into subjection; lest that by any means, when I have preached to others, I myself should be a castaway."

He pursues a certain course of life in order that he may not be a castaway—not be disapproved.

Now it was God that was to approve or disapprove of him, for he says, "It is a very small thing that I should be judged of you or of man's judgment; * * he that judgeth me is the Lord." (1 Cor. iv:3, 4.)

When was this approval or disapproval to occur? It was to occur after Paul had preached to others. Lest (keeruxas) *having preached*, the preaching is considered as past. Now Paul's preaching continued, and he expected it to continue until his death.

Therefore as the preaching was to continue until death, and the decision was to be rendered after the preaching was finished, it follows that the decision was to be rendered after the death of the apostle. And thus by his conduct and belief the apostle teaches that there is a judgment after death.

The same truth is taught in Heb. x:28, 29: "He that despised Moses' law died without mercy under two or three witnesses; of how much sorer punishment, suppose ye, shall he be thought worthy who hath trodden under foot the Son of God, and counted the blood of the covenant, wherewith he was sanctified, an unholy thing, and hath done despite unto the Spirit of grace?"

The punishment of the contemners of the blood of the new covenant, and despisers of the Spirit of grace is to be *sorer* than death " without mercy." And this punishment is sure to come, for " vengeance belongeth unto me; I will recompense, saith the Lord." (Heb. x:30.) Now it is a matter of common observation that the above mentioned sinners do not in this life experience a punishment sorer than death without mercy. Multitudes of them are in the enjoyment of so much earthly comfort as to prefer their condition by far to that of death without mercy. And thus they continue until death comes. Therefore, as their punishment is to be sorer than death without mercy, it must be meted out to them subsequent to their physical death.

The same truth is taught in Heb. ix:27,28. "And as it is appointed unto the men once to die, but after this, judgment; so the Christ was once offered to bear the sins of many, and unto them that look for him shall he appear the second time, without sin unto salvation."

Inasmuch as some Universalists claim that the insertion of the article before "men," which is omitted in the English version, would be in their favor, we have inserted it as above. We have also inserted the article, which in the Greek occurs before Christ, just as above. Now it seems plainly evident that the writer inserts the article before both "men" and "Christ" to indicate that these parties are considered as possessing a relation to each other. He says: "As the men die once, so the Christ was offered once. Now since the object of the article is to indicate the existence of a relation between these two parties, therefore, the "men," so far as the force of the article is concerned, may be as numerous as the men for whom Christ died. For a relation certainly exists between Christ and all for whom he died."

On this passage "The Ambassador" (April 6, 1867), says: "The Universalist exposition in brief is this: The men appointed to die were * * the priests under the law; the death was by proxy, * * and the judgment which followed was to justification, not to condemnation. * * And for *an analogous purpose* that of justification and redemption, Christ, the High Priest of the new covenant, was 'appointed' to die to bear the sins of many. Such an exposition *accords with the scope of the chapter*, and it gives a meaning to the words 'as' and 'so' in the passage. But the orthodox exposition violently wrenches the passage away from the scope of the chapter, and makes meaningless the two words named."

Rev. J. M. Austin (Debate on Endless Punishment, p. 658), thus understands the passage: " As it is appointed unto men (Jewish High Priests) once to die (once a year to die sacrificially), but after this the judgment (*i. e.*, the decision which they brought from God of approbation or disapprobation of the proceedings of the Jews), so Christ was once offered to bear the sins of many.

Thus both the death (which is not real but figurative) and the subsequent judgment are affirmed to consist solely of the events of the Jewish temple service. The Orthodox, on the other hand, consider the "men" to be men in general; the death, physical; and the judgment one which occurs subsequent to physical death.

Let us now test the agreement of these two interpretations with our passage.

It is plain from the passage and both parties are agreed, that "the men" are appointed to die once, and that the Christ was offered once; that the judgment occurs after the death of the men, and that the Christ is to appear unto salvation after his physical death. Let us now incorporate into the sentence such words as will make it undeniably assert the orthodox interpretation; and notice the result. And as it is appointed unto men in general to die once physically, but after this death there is judgment, so Christ was once offered to bear the sins of many, and shall appear unto them that look for him the second time, without sin, unto salvation."

Here the words "as" and "so" are not meaningless since they perform the same office as in the passage, Heb. ix:27, 28. In that passage they are used to introduce a resemblance between the death of the men, and the death of Christ. And that resemblance consists in the fact that each death occurs once, and no more than once. In the sentence which we have so shaped as to accord with the orthodox understanding of the passage. they are used to introduce a resemblance between the death of men and the death of Christ. And that resemblance consists in the fact that each occurs once, and no more than once. Their use in the two sentences is the same. The fact that the orthodox exposition asserts a judgment after the death of the men, makes no difference in regard to the use of the two words, since Heb. ix:27, 28 also asserts a judgment after the death of the men. Neither does the fact that the judgment brings danger, and Christ's appearing brings rescue from danger—and that these are opposites—make any difference in regard to the use of the two words, since in the parallel of I Cor. xv:22, "As in Adam all die, even so in Christ shall all be made alive," the death in Adam and the life in Christ are opposites.

Let us now endeavor to ascertain whether the statements of the orthodox exposition are in accordance with truth.. The one death of men—the one death of Christ—the appearing of Christ after his death for the salvation of his people—no Christian will deny. Now, if the other statement—the danger after death of condemnation before God—be denied, then all those who deny that danger are compelled because of that denial to abandon all proof of salvation after death, so far as that proof is drawn from the work which God has assigned to Christ. For it is as plain as the light of day that if there be no danger of condemnation beyond physical death, then Christ cannot save from condemnation beyond physical death.

Salvation necessarily implies a danger from which to be saved. This dilemma then presents itself to Universalists. After physical death there is a danger from which Christ saves men, or there is not. If there be, then all the statements of the Orthodox exposition are in accordance with truth. If there be not, then Christ saves no man after physical death; and Universalists must relinquish all hope of, and argument for, a final salvation through Christ. And since the only final salvation which the Bible teaches, is that which comes through Christ, they must also discard the Bible itself as furnishing proof of a final salvation. But since Universalists do hold that the Bible furnishes proof of a final salvation, they must therefore admit the danger of condemnation in a judgment subsequent to death. Thus they must admit that all the four statements of the Orthodox exposition are true. And if these statements be admitted to be true, then it matters nothing at all in the controversy whether the one exposition or the other be correct; since the only purpose for which the passage is introduced, is to show that a certain one of those statements is true.

Let us now attend to the Universalist exposition, and see whether it preserves the resemblance introduced by "as" and "so." As has already been stated, it is plain from the passage, and both parties are agreed, that the men are said to die once, and the Christ is said to be offered once. The resemblance then is, that each event spoken of occurs once.

Notice now how the writer of the Hebrews dwells on the fact that Christ's offering was made once, and no more than once. In verse 12 he says: "Neither by the blood of goats and calves, but by his own blood, he entered in once into the holy place." In verse 26, " But now once in the end of the world hath he appeared to put away sin by the sacrifice of himself." In verse 28, "So Christ was once offered to bear the sins of many." In chapter 10, verse 10, he says: " By the which will we are sanctified through the offering of the body of Jesus Christ once." In v. 12, " But this man after he had offered one sacrifice for sins forever sat down on the right hand of God." In v. 14, "For by one offering he hath perfected forever them that are sanctified." Now, from these repeated affirmations, one can not avoid seeing that according to the mind of the writer Christ was offered in sacrifice but once. And since the writer represents Christ as being offered but once, he must also be regarded as representing in the resemblance "the men" as dying but once, thus: As the men die but once, so the Christ was offered but once. And should the writer's own statements make it evident that he considers the offering of the High Priests as being made not once only but often, then it is plainly manifest that he would not and could not consistently represent the Christ in being offered once as resembling the High Priests in their being offered often. Since "once" and "often" are not similar, but dissimilar.

Now, the writer's own statements do plainly show that he considers the offering of the High Priest as being made not once only, but often.

He says (x 1–3) just after the passage in consideration: "For the law * * can never with those sacrifices which they offered year by year continually, make the comers thereunto perfect. For then would they not have ceased to be offered? because that the worshipers once purged should have no more conscience of sins. But in those sacrifices there is a remembrance again made of sins every year."

Just before the passage in consideration he says (vs. 25, 26), "Nor yet that he (Christ) should offer himself often as the high priest entereth into the holy place every year with blood of others; for then must he often have suffered since the foundation of the world." These affirmations of the writer of Hebrews prove beyond all doubt that he considers the offering of the High Priest as occurring not once but often. And since he does so consider he would not, and could not consistently, represent the Christ in being offered once as resembling the High Priests in their being offered often. For "once" and "often" are not similar but dissimilar. Who can tell the office which "as" and "so" serve in the following sentence—"As it is appointed unto the High Priests to die often, so Christ was offered once." And yet if "the men" signify "the High Priests," we must suppose that the inspired author of Hebrews considered as legitimate such a sentence and resemblance as that.

That "the men" do not signify Jewish High

Priests may also be shown by another method. If "men" stands for "High Priests" more than one High Priest must of course be meant. High Priests in succession from the institution of the Levitical Priesthood down to the sacrifice of Christ, must be intended. And since but one High Priest officiated at a single offering, more than one High Priest implies of necessity that the offering is made more than once. And since the Levitical High Priesthood existed some fifteen hundred years previous to the death of Christ, and for nearly the whole of that time offered the yearly offering, that offering was of course repeated nearly fifteen hundred times.

Now when the design of the author was to state a resemblance to the Christ offered but once, who can see the reasonableness of his saying "men" instead of "man," or "High Priests" instead of "High Priest," so long as the officiating of more than one High Priest makes certain a repetition of the offering and thus destroys its power to furnish a resemblance to the Christ as offered but once. Restricted to a single High Priest and a single year, the offering of the High Priest would occur but once; and might be used to furnish a resemblance to the once offering of the Christ; but cannot be so used when reference is had to more High Priests than one or to more years than one. Our Universalist friends appear to forget that "once every year" and "year by year continually" mean twice in two years and a thousand times in a thousand years.

Still further, no one would think of claiming that the offering of Christ but once, finds a resemblance in the daily offering of the ordinary priests; and yet our writer when expressly pointing out the meaning of the once a year offering of the High Priest in distinction from the daily offering of the ordinary priests, so far from giving any hint that the once a year offering of the High Priest typifies the Christ as offered once, does affirm it to teach an entirely different truth, viz.: "The Holy Ghost this signifying that the way into the holiest of all was not yet made manifest while as the first tabernacle was yet standing." (ix:6-8.) Now when the writer himself affirms the meaning of the once a year offering, by what right do men affirm that it has a different meaning?

Let us now notice whether anything in the course of thought demands that "the men" shall be understood to signify "High Priests." Verses 2-5 mention the making of the tabernacle, and the articles which it contained. Vs. 6-10 describe the priestly service and assert the inefficacy of the sacrifices "as pertaining to the conscience." Vs. 11-28, in which is contained the passage under consideration, teach the superiority and efficacy of the sacrifice of Christ. Now we can see nothing in this course and terminus of thought—the scope—that forbids the writer to mention the analogy existing between the one death of men and the one offering of Christ. The design is to set forth the power and the grandeur of Christ's one sacrifice. And we ask if the one death of the untold millions for whom the Christ did die does not furnish a nobler and more suitable parallel to that one and grandly efficacious sacrifice, than the once a year by proxy death of Jewish High Priests? The once a year by proxy death, as the writer affirms, must be repeated from its very weakness. But the one death of men is of such power that no strength but God's can subdue it. And since God was in Christ subduing death, the apostle most fitly indicates the analogy between Christ's one sacrifice and the men's one death.

Paul teaches the same truth in Phil. iii:18, 19; "For many walk of whom I have told you often, and now tell you even weeping, that they are the enemies of the cross of Christ. Whose end is destruction, whose God is their belly, and whose glory is in their shame, who mind earthly things."

The "*end*" here spoken of must be either the termination of the earthly life, or the sad destiny of these enemies beyond the grave.

It cannot be the simple termination of the earthly life, for then since believers also die God would visit with the same treatment even in the earthly life, the enemies of the cross and true disciples; a supposition which the advocates of the final salvation of all are by no means willing to allow. It cannot be the violent and speedy termination of the earthly life; for this multitudes of the early Christians experienced, and even because of their love to Jesus. And therefore it must be the destiny of these enemies beyond the grave. The end of these enemies beyond the grave the apostle affirms to be destruction.

The teachings of the Saviour respecting the destroyed cities also prove a judgment after death. He says, Mark vi:11 : "Whosoever shall not receive you, nor hear you, when ye depart thence, shake off the dust under your feet for a testimony against them. Verily I say unto you, It shall be more tolerable for Sodom and Gomorrah in the day of judgment, than for that city."

The teaching of a judgment after death is here so plain that it seems as if all but the wilfully blind must see it. Two things are here to be noted. The first, that the judgment of which Christ speaks is future to the time of his speaking, "It shall be." The second, that the Saviour includes in that judgment the inhabitants of Sodom and Gomorrah, "It shall be more tolerable for Sodom and Gomorrah." Now these cities were destroyed by fire from heaven 1900 years previous to the time of Christ's speaking; and even if it be supposed that some of the wicked inhabitants by any means escaped that destruction, surely not even the advocates of a universal restoration will claim that these escaped ones lived through the long 1900 years, and were still to be judged in the earthly life subsequent to the time in which Christ spake. All were dead then at the time of Christ's speaking, and yet subsequent to that speaking they were still to come into judgment. This clearly teaches a judgment after death.

Proposition IV. The Scriptures teach that Christ will come personally and visibly to judge the nations; a coming to judgment such as has not yet taken place, such as does not take place in the ordinary earthly life, and which is yet, perhaps, humanly speaking, in the distant future.

Some forty days after his resurrection Christ ascended into heaven. We are to show first, the fact of his personal and visible coming.

In Christ's last personal interview with his disciples he spake unto them as follows: "It is not for you to know the times or the seasons which the Father hath put in his power. But ye shall receive power after that the Holy Ghost is come upon you ; and ye shall be witnesses unto me both in Jerusalem, and in all Judea, and in all Samaria, and unto the uttermost parts of the earth." And when he had spoken these things, "while they beheld, he was taken up and a cloud received him out of their sight .And while they looked steadfastly toward heaven as he went up, behold two men stood by them in white apparel, which also said, Ye men of Galilee, why stand ye gazing up into heaven? This same Jesus which is taken up from you into heaven shall so come in like manner as ye have seen him go into heaven." (Acts i:9-11.)

No one should doubt that this account teaches Christ's personal and visible return from heaven.

The same truth is also taught in Acts iii: 19-21. "Repent ye, therefore, and be converted, that your sins may be blotted out, when the times of refreshing shall come from the presence of the Lord; and he shall send Jesus Christ which before was preached unto you; whom the heavens must receive until the times of restitution of all things, which God hath spoken by the mouth of all his holy prophets since the world began. That is—from the heavens which now receive him God will send Christ at the times of restitution. This can be spoken of nothing but his personal coming. Olshausen (*in loco*) remarks: " The coming of Christ * * * (parousia) is to be conceived as coinciding with the times of refreshing, and his sojourn in the heavenly world closes with his return to the earth for the completion of his work."

We now proceed to show that this personal coming of Christ will result in his approving and blessing his believing people.

The apostle Peter teaches as follows: "An inheritance incorruptible and undefiled, and that fadeth not away, reserved in heaven for you who are kept by the power of God through faith unto salvation ready to be revealed in the last time: wherein ye greatly rejoice though now for a season (if need be) ye are in heaviness through manifold temptations, that the trial of your faith, though it be tried with fire, might be found unto praise, and honor and glory at the appearing of Jesus Christ, whom not having seen ye love." (I Pet. i:4-7.)

The same apostle further says: "Feed the flock of God which is among you, taking the oversight thereof not by constraint, but willingly, not for filthy lucre, but of a ready mind; neither as being lords over God's heritage, but being ensamples to the flock: and when the chief Shepherd shall appear, ye shall receive a crown of glory that fadeth not away." (I Pet. v:2-4.)

Notice here two things: 1st. The meaning of the word translated "appear." 2d. That those spoken of receive, at that "appearing," a crown of glory that fadeth not away.

1. The word translated "appear."

The same word occurs in the following passages: Mark iv:22: "For there is nothing hid which shall not be *manifested*—made to appear."

Mark xvi:12. "After that he (Jesus), *appeared* in another form unto two of them as they walked and went into the country." This appearance was after Christ's resurrection.

Mark xvi;14: "Afterward he *appeared* unto the eleven as they sat at meat and upbraided them with their unbelief and hardness of heart, because they believed not them which had seen him after he was risen."

John vii:4: "There is no man that doeth anything in secret and he himself seeketh to be known openly; if thou do these things *show* thyself to the world." In this verse the word translated "show" is the same as above (I Pet. v:4) translated "appear."

John xxi:1. "After these things Jesus *showed* himself (made himself appear) again to the disciples at the Sea of Tiberias; and on this wise *showed* he himself" (made himself appear).

John xxi:14: "This is now the third time that Jesus showed himself (made himself appear) to his disciples after that he was risen from the dead."

II Cor. v:10: "We must all appear before the judgment seat of Christ."

I Tim. iii:16: "God was *manifest* (made to appear) in the flesh, justified in the Spirit, seen of angels, preached unto the Gentiles, believed on in the world, received up into glory." That is, God appeared in the flesh in the person of Christ.

Heb. ix:26: "But now once in the end of the world hath he (Christ) *appeared* to put away sin by the sacrifice of himself."

I John iii:5: "And ye know that he (Christ) was *manifested* (made to appear) to take away our sins; and in him is no sin."

I John iii:8: "For this purpose the Son of God was manifested (made to appear) that he might destroy the works of the devil."

In all these passages the appearance of Christ is considered as a visible appearance, and it makes the conviction very strong that the appearance mentioned in I Pet. v:4 is also considered as visible. Indeed, we venture the assertion without fear of successful contradiction, that the word translated in I Pet. v:4 "appear," is never in the New Testament applied to a "person," a human being, without that person is considered as visibly appearing.

We now proceed to notice the second thing mentioned, viz.: That those spoken of receive at that appearing "a crown of glory that fadeth not away."

And on this we remark: That the manner in which the apostle addresses them in other parts of the epistle shows clearly that he did not consider them as possessing, nor as about to possess in this earthly life, the unfading crown of glory.

1. He tells them that their "inheritance incorruptible, and that fadeth not away" is "reserved in heaven" for them. Now as neither the inheritance nor the crown of glory is to fade away, it follows that the duration of the one must be as lasting as that of the other. And as the "inheritance" is "in heaven" and is as lasting as "heaven," therefore the "crown of glory" is also as lasting as heaven. And of necessary consequence it must be enjoyed in the life to come.

2. Instead of the apostle considering glory in the earthly life as unfading, he tells them, "All flesh is as grass, and all the glory of man as the flower of grass. The grass withereth, and the flower thereof falleth away." (I Pet. i:24.)

3. When the crown of unfading glory shall be received by Christ's people it is but reasonable to suppose that all their bitter suffering is past; yet the apostle addresses them as yet to suffer. He says (I Pet. iv:1): "Forasmuch then as Christ hath suffered for us in the flesh, arm yourselves likewise with the same mind." They are yet to wear their armor. The fight is not over, and the crown is not yet won.

Also (iv:12, 13.) "Beloved, think it not

strange concerning the fiery trial which is to try you as though some strange thing happened unto you; but rejoice inasmuch as ye are partakers of Christ's sufferings; that when his glory shall be revealed ye may be glad also with exceeding joy." Also (iv:19), "Let them that suffer according to the will of God, commit the keeping of their souls unto Him in well doing, as unto a faithful Creator."

Also, (v : 9,) " Resist (the devil) steadfast in the faith, knowing that the same afflictions are accomplished in your brethren that are in the world. But the God of all grace, who hath called us unto his eternal glory by Christ Jesus, *after that ye have suffered awhile*, make you perfect, establish, strengthen, settle you."

These statements clearly show that the apostle did not consider them as possessing in this earthly life, the crown of glory.

2. God dealt doubtless on the same principle with the Christians whom Peter addressed, as he did with Paul and the Christians in Corinth, whom Paul addressed. *After* Paul's course was finished, and the time of departure (from earth) was at hand, his " crown of righteousness" was not even yet given him, but was still " laid up" and to be given at a future day—the day of the appearing of the Lord, the righteous Judge. And if we believe that God gave the Christians

whom Peter addresed, their "crown" in this life, and "laid up" Paul's until the future life, must we not also believe that he dealt more favorably with the one than with the other party?

But as Paul's full reward and Christ's full reward were both reserved by the Father until the next life, there is no reason whatever for supposing that he dealt in different manner with the Christian "strangers scattered throughout Pontus, Galatia, Cappadocia, Asia and Bithynia."

Now each of these two facts which have just been clearly proved—that Christ gives the "crown" at his visible appearing, and that Christians receive not the crown until the present earthly life is past, leaves no escape from the conclusion that the crown of unfading glory is not worn in this present earthly life.

We present one more passage in which the word translated *appear* occurs; and which passage without doubt refers to Christ's visible appearance.

I John, iii:2, "Beloved, now are we the sons of God, and it doth not yet appear what we shall be; but we know that when he shall *appear*, we shall be like him; for we shall see him as he is."

Notice here two things:

1. The visibility of his appearance.

"When he shall appear * * we shall see him as he is." This is as plain as words can make it.

2. "The time of the appearance."

(*a*) It is future to the time of the apostle's writing.

"When he shall appear." (1) The tense is future. (2) A contrast is also made between the present and future condition of those whom he addresses.

Now are we the sons of God, what we shall be doth not yet appear.

(3) This appearance with its result, was hoped for, not realized, v. 3.

(*b*) It does not occur until the termination of the earthly life.

Shown, 1. At that appearance we shall see him as he is. Now during the continuance of the earthly life, no believer sees him as he is. He has experienced the resurrection of the body and is now in glory.

2. At that visible and glorious appearing, we shall be like him. Like him we shall possess the glorious resurrection body. This of course is not possessed in the present earthly life.

We continue our proofs of Christ's visible appearance.

Phil. iii: 20, 21. " For our conversation is in heaven; from whence also we look for the Saviour, the Lord Jesus Christ; who shall change our vile body, that it may be fashioned like unto his glorious body."

He looked for Christ to come from heaven, because on Christ's coming, Paul's vile body would be fashioned like unto Christ's glorious body.

This coming of Christ and the change of Paul's vile body did not, of course take place during Paul's earthly life. The change is the one produced in the resurrection of the just.

Heb. ix: 28, " Christ was once offered to bear the sins of many; and unto them that look for him shall he appear the second time, without sin unto salvation."

There is a contrast here between Christ's second and first appearing. And but two appearings are thought of—not multitudes of appearings.

The first appearing, none will deny, was in his earthly life; when and at the close of which, he was once offered to bear the sins of many. Now this first was a visible appearing. And as he is to appear the second time unto them that look for him, this second appearance, we may very properly conclude, will also be visible. It will be without sin unto salvation; of course the salvation of his people, that full salvation which introduces them into the glories of the resurrection state.

I Thess. ii : 19, " What is our hope, or joy, or crown of rejoicing? Are not even ye in the presence of our Lord Jesus Christ at his coming?"

This verse indicates that the apostles expected to be in company with the Christians of Thessalonica at the coming of Jesus Christ; and thus excludes the idea that the coming of Christ is immediately subsequent to the death of believers. Paul died at Rome, and it cannot be thought that all or the majority of the believers at Thessalonica, were gathered together and martyred with him at Rome. It leads to the thought of the simultaneous resurrection and gathering together of believers that sleep in Jesus. " Behold, I show you a mystery, we shall not all sleep, but we shall all be changed, in a moment, in the twinkling of an eye, at the last trump, for the trumpet shall sound, and the dead shall be raised incorruptible." (I Cor. xv : 51, 52).

I Thess. iii : 13, " Abound in love * * to the end that he may establish your hearts unblamable in holiness before God, even our Father, at the coming of our Lord Jesus Christ with all his saints."

This coming certainly has not yet taken place, does not take place at the death of each individual believer; and will not take place until the close of the gospel dispensation, when the dead in Christ shall rise.

This coming is also to be attended with blessing to obedient believers. Their hearts are to be established "unblamable in holiness before God."

Titus ii:12, 13. "We should live soberly, righteously and godly in this present world; looking for that blessed hope, and the glorious appearing of the great God, and our Saviour Jesus Christ."

1. This appearing did not occur at the destruction of Jerusalem, for it was to be looked for by the Christians at Crete. Both Christ and Paul wept over the unhappy fate of the Jews.

2. If not at Jerusalem it is still in the future, for the history of the church gives no account of "the glorious appearing" or "the appearing of the glory" of the great God, and our Saviour Jesus Christ, since the writing of the epistle.

3. If it is to be a "glorious appearing" and to be looked for, it will be visible. And if it is to be the appearing of the Saviour Jesus Christ to living men it will be visible.

Col. iii:4. "When Christ who is our life shall appear, then shall ye also appear with him in glory."

This is either : 1st. Christ's appearance to the individual believer just after physical death, or 2d, and more probably, the appearance of Christ attended by the glorified bodies of resurrected believers. This is to occur at the close of the gospel dispensation and to be immediately followed by the glorious resurrection change in the bodies of living believers.

Proposition V. The Scriptures teach such a visible coming of Christ as results in the bodily resurrection of the dead in Christ, in the bodily transformation of living believers, and in painful judgments on the ungodly; and as such is of course distinct from his coming at the destruction of Jerusalem, distinct from his coming in ordinary temporal judgments, and distinct from his coming at the hour of physical death.

In support of the above proposition we offer the following proofs: I Thess. iv:13-17: " I would not have you to be ignorant, brethren, concerning them which are asleep, that ye sorrow not even as others which have no hope. For if we believe that Jesus died and rose again, even so them also which sleep in Jesus will God bring with him. For this we say unto you by the word of the Lord, that we which are alive and remain unto the coming of the Lord, shall not prevent (precede) them which are asleep. For the Lord himself shall descend from heaven with a shout, with the voice of the archangel, and with the trump of God; and the dead in Christ shall rise first; then we which are alive and remain shall be caught up together with them in the clouds to meet the Lord in the air; and so shall we ever be with the Lord."

This is very decisive as to the bodily resurrection of the "dead in Christ" at "*the coming* of the Lord." It also implies the resurrection change of living believers. For they are to "be caught up together with them in the clouds, to meet the Lord in the air," and so to be ever with the Lord. This change of believers at Christ's coming is very clearly taught in I Cor. xv:50-52: "Flesh and blood cannot inherit the kingdom of God. We shall not all sleep, but we shall all be changed, in a moment, in the twinkling of an eye, at the last trump; for the trumpet shall sound, and the dead shall be raised incorruptible, and we shall be changed."

This clearly teaches the resurrection change of living believers at the visible coming of Christ.

Now the proof is to be given that this visible coming of Christ will result in painful judgments on the ungodly.

In I Thess. iv:13-17, as has just been said, Paul teaches the resurrection of the dead in Christ. In the fifth chapter he continues as follows: "But of the times and seasons, brethren, ye have no need that I write unto you. For yourselves know perfectly that the day of the Lord so cometh as a thief in the night. For when they shall say peace and safety, then sudden destruction cometh upon them, as travail upon a woman with child, and they shall not escape."

The day of the Lord, here mentioned, is the time when "the Lord himself shall descend from heaven with a shout, and with the trumpof God," as the connection of the thought clearly shows. He has just told of the descending of the Lord from heaven and that they could comfort one another with these words. Then he speaks of "the day of the Lord," and most certainly he means by this, the day of the Lord's descent from heaven.

Notice further that this day of the Lord brings with it destruction. "The day of the Lord cometh as a thief in the night. For when they shall say, Peace and safety, then sudden destruction cometh upon them."

The apostle here evidently connects with the coming of the day of the Lord, a sudden destruction. Otherwise there is no force in the reason which the apostle presents.

If it should be said, The days of the Lord came in times of old with great severity, because the citizens of Sodom and the antediluvians were dealt with with great severity, then it necessarily follows that the times of those severe dealings were the days of the Lord.

If it should be said, The hour of the teacher came unexpectedly, because the child was punished unexpectedly, then it necessarily follows that the punishing of the child, or the time of that punishing was the hour of the teacher. So if it should be said, The day of the Lord comes unexpectedly, because suffering comes unexpectedly, then suffering, or the time of suffering, must be the day of the Lord. So, if it should be said, The day of the Lord comes unexpectedly, because sudden destruction comes on them unexpectedly, then the sudden destruction or the time of that destruction must be the day of the Lord. But this is just what is said, not in words but in meaning. For both the coming of the thief, and the coming of the sudden destruction, are unexpected. Therefore the time in which this sudden destruction comes is the day of the Lord.

Another proof is contained in II Thess. i: 6-10: "Seeing it is a righteous thing with God to recompense tribulation to them that trouble you; and to you who are troubled rest with us when the Lord Jesus shall be revealed from heaven with his mighty angels, in flaming fire taking vengeance on them that know not God, and that obey not the gospel of our Lord Jesus Christ; who shall be punished with everlasting destruction from the presence of the Lord, and from the glory of his power; when he shall come to be glorified in his saints, and to be admired in all them that believe."

This passage teaches the infliction of painful judgments on the ungodly. The only question here is, as to the time in which these judgments occur.

Is the time the destruction of Jerusalem, or is it a still future and visible coming of Christ to judgment?

Let us notice some points which have a bearing on this question.

1. At the time of the revealing of the Lord Jesus from heaven the afflicted believers at Thessalonica are to have "rest with us," that is with Paul; for Paul is certainly included in the "us." Now it is a well known fact that Paul was put to death by being beheaded some years before the destruction of Jerusalem. And if the afflicted believers were recompensed at Jerusalem's destruction with rest with Paul, it could only have been by means of their physical death. For Paul was dead. Now should the very improbable supposition that the Thessalonian Christians died at the time of Jerusalem's destruction, be admitted, we ask, what worse thing happened as tribulation to those multitudes of wicked Jews at Jerusalem who are killed, and suddenly, in battle? And the answer must be, "No worse." But this makes the tribulation and the rest, things equally desirable, which is absurd. And therefore the supposition — that the afflicted believers of Thessalonica received rest with Paul at the destruction of Jerusalem—must be incorrect, since it conducts to an absurd conclusion. But if that supposition be incorrect, then it necessarily follows that the revealing of the Lord Jesus from heaven, spoken of in the above passage, did not occur at the destruction of Jerusalem.

II. Those on whom vengeance is to be taken " when the Lord Jesus shall be revealed from heaven," are they that know not God and obey not the gospel of our Lord Jesus Christ. Not a hint is here of nationality. The reference is alone to individual character. Now it is certain that at the destruction of Jerusalem, the great majority of the Gentiles possessed the character referred to. They were idolators—they obeyed not the gospel. And centuries yet after Jerusalem's destruction, the Roman empire was under idolatrous control. And scattered over the earth the wicked Gentiles far outnumbered the wicked Jews. Now as the reference is alone to character it seems unreasonable to suppose that when judgment comes, and comes *especially* because of character, the great majority of those possessing that character, shall be excluded from the judgment. And if the judgment occurred at Jerusalem, the great majority were most certainly so excluded. For but a very small part of the wicked Gentiles were gathered at Jerusalem.

III. The apostle teaches that when Christ comes he "is to be admired in all them that believe."

He limits the "all" by "them that believe." Now in order to harmonize this statement with the belief that this coming was realized in the destruction of Jerusalem, one of two things must be done :

Either deceased believers must be included in the all of them that believe, or the limitation of the apostle must be still further limited, making all them that believe, to mean only a part of "them that believe." Now Christ is represented as *coming* to be admired ; and there is no propriety in representing Christ as coming to be admired in or by deceased believers, unless with such coming there is connected the resurrection of such believers. And as no such resurrection occurred at the destruction of Jerusalem, the idea that dead and unresurrected believers are included in the "all them that believe," must be abandoned.

Further: At the time of Jerusalem's destruction, telegraphs, and steamboats and railroads were unknown, and as a consequence of the imperfect means of communicating information, it was spread among the nations quite slowly. Now subsequent to the destruction of the city, and before the knowledge of that destruction would reach "all them that believe," some of them that believe would die. And as a consequence, "all" of them that believed when Jerusalem was destroyed, can only mean "a part" of them that believed when Jerusalem was destroyed. The apostle's limitation must be still further limited.

IV. The manner in which the apostle exhorts them not to be shaken in mind, or troubled, as that the day of Christ is at hand; opposes the idea that that day came at the destruction of Jerusalem.

He beseeches by the coming of our Lord Jesus Christ, and *our gathering together* unto *him*.

Here the apostle evidently implies a connection between the coming of Christ, and " our gathering" (*i. e.* of believers) unto him. And the gathering together unto Christ, seems also to mean a gathering unto him as a person. Now at the destruction of Jerusalem, instead of a gathering together, there was rather a scattering abroad. Christ says (Matt. xxiv:15, 16, 20): "When ye shall see the abomination of desolation, spoken of by Daniel the prophet, stand in the holy place, * * then let them which be in Judea flee into the mountains." " Pray ye that your *flight* be not in the winter." And since Christ did not come personally at the destruction of Jerusalem, there was of course no gathering together unto him as a person.

Now since there was no gathering either of Thessalonian believers, or of believers in general at the dstruction of Jerusalem, and since the apostle connects such gathering with the coming of Christ, therefore, the coming of Christ did not take place at the destruction of that city. This gathering together unto Christ is yet in the future, and will take place when "the dead in Christ shall rise first," and " we which are alive and remain shall be caught up together with them in the clouds, to meet the Lord in the air." (I Thess. iv:16, 17.)

V. The fact that the salvation which believers experience in the day of the Lord, is not limited to this life, opposes the idea that that day occurred at the destruction of Jerusalem.

That such is the fact is plainly shown by the connection of thought. "The day of the Lord so cometh as a thief in the night. For when they shall say peace and safety, their sudden destruction comes." "Ye brethren are not in darkness, that that day should overtake you as a thief. Ye are all the children of light, and the children of the day. Let us who are of the day be sober, putting on the breastplate of faith and love, and for a helmet the hope of salvation, for God hath not appointed us to wrath, but to obtain salvation by our Lord Jesus Christ. (I Thess. v: 2-9). Now it is very evident that the salvation here spoken of is salvation in the day of the Lord. They should act as children of light, because God has appointed them to salvation. And that this salvation extends beyond this present life, the next verse clearly shows: "To obtain salvation by our Lord Jesus Christ who died for us that, whether we wake or sleep, we should live together with him."

Those who sleep in Christ are also in experiencing this salvation to live together with Christ, and therefore the salvation can not be limited to the earthly life. But the salvation experienced by believers at the destruction of Jerusalem was limited to this life, and since the salvation experienced at the destruction of that city, was not the salvation which believers are to experience in the day of the Lord, therefore "the day of the Lord" did not occur at the destruction of that city.

VI. The fact that certain events foretold by the apostle as to occur either before or in the day of the Lord, had not occurred when the destruction of Jerusalem was completed, proves that the destruction of that city was not "the day of the Lord."

Paul says: "Be not soon shaken in mind as that the day of Christ is at hand.

Let no man deceive you by any means; for that day shall not come except there come a falling away first, and that man of sin be revealed, the son of perdition, who opposeth and exalteth himself above all that is called God, or that is worshiped; so that he as God sitteth in the temple of God, showing himself that he is God. * * * Whose coming is after the working of Satan with all power and signs and lying wonders, and with all deceivableness of unrighteousness." (II Thess. ii : 2-4, 9, 10).

The man of sin, as God, sitteth in the temple of God. The temple of God is not the temple at Jerusalem, but the Christian Church. When the sacrifice of Christ was offered on the cross, the veil of the temple was rent in twain—rent by the agency of God himself—and thus it was manifested that the temple had served its purpose, and was henceforth to be considered the temple of God no more. That the Christian Church is the temple of God, is proved by the apostle's language in other epistles. In I Cor iii :16, he says: " Know ye not that ye are the temple of God, and that the Spirit of God dwelleth in you. If any man defile the temple of God him shall God destroy; for the temple of God is holy, which temple ye are."

And in II Cor. vi:16, "And what agreement hath the temple of God with idols? for ye are the temple of the living God." The man of sin then when revealed is to come forth from the Christian church. He is further to sit in the temple of God showing himself that he is God. And also his coming is after the working of Satan with all power and signs and lying wonders.

Now up to the time of Jerusalem's complete destruction there was nothing that can be considered a fulfilment of these inspired predictions.

The early Christians who lived subsequent to Jerusalem's destruction, believed that the revealing of the man of sin was yet in the future, and that it would not occur until the destruction of the then Roman empire. Tertullian says in his apology, "We Christians are under a particular necessity of praying for the emperors, and for the continued state of the empire, because we know the dreadful power which hangs over the whole world; and the conclusion of the age, which threatens the most horrible evils, is retarded by the continuance of the time appointed for the Roman empire. We pray therefore that this evil may be deferred by the perpetuity of the state." And Jerome, after Rome was taken by the Goths, says: "He which restrained is now taken away, and hence we understand that Antichrist is near." (Hill's Lectures in Divinity, p. 713).

Justin Martyr, of the second century, says: "He who is about to speak blasphemous and audacious things against the Most High is already at the doors, whose continuance Daniel signifies to be for a time, times, and half a time. He (Christ) shall come with glory from the heavens, when also the man of apostacy speaking great words against the Highest, will dare to do wicked things against us Christians."

Irenæus, also of the second century, says: "When Antichrist, reigning three years and six months, shall have laid waste all things in this world, and have sat in the temple of Jerusalem, then shall the Lord come from heaven in the clouds, casting Antichrist and them that obey him into the lake of fire, but bringing to the just the times of the kingdom."

Cyprian, of the third century, says: "We are now in the end and consummation of the world—the fatal time of Antichrist is at hand."

Ambrose, of the fourth century, says: "The abomination of desolation is the abominable advent of Antichrist, who with ill-omened sacrilege will defile the inner chambers of men's minds, and will sit literally in the temple, usurping the throne of divine power. Then will come desolation, seeing that most will fall away from true religion, and lapse into error: then will come the day of the Lord."

Augustine, on II Thess. ii, says: "No one doubts that the apostle said these things of Antichrist, and that the day of judgment, which he here calls 'the day of the Lord,' will not come unless he whom he calls an apostate, that is to say from the Lord God, shall first come."

Chrysostom, Bishop of Constantinople in the fourth century, says: "As Rome succeeded Greece, so Antichrist is to succeed Rome; and Christ our Saviour, Antichrist." (The Voice of the Church, pp. 93, 295, 296, 298, 300.)

Dr. Olshausen, of Germany, while admitting that the destruction of Jerusalem may be a type of the evils in the time of the revealing of the man of sin, yet teaches that that revealing is yet future. He says: "If we after this turn to the critical examinations of these various opinions upon Antichrist, and upon what detains him, we must by all means lay it down as an axiom that every interpretation is false which admits the apostle's representation to be exhausted in any representation of the past. For according to his express declaration, Christ's coming, and with it the resurrection of the faithful, and the kingdom of God are immediately to follow on the coming of the falling away, and of Antichrist. Now, as up to this time nothing of that has happened, the coming of Antichrist also can only be considered as something future." (Com. II Thes. ii: 7.)

We close this part of our subject with the testimony of the learned theologian, Prof. Charles Hodge, D. D. He says (Systematic Theology, Vol. III, p. 836): "According, then, to the common faith of the church, the three great events which are to precede the second advent of Christ, are the universal proclamation of the Gospel on the conversion of the Gentile world, the national conversion of the Jews, and the appearance of Antichrist."

And inasmuch as these three great events have not even yet occurred, of course the advent of the Lord did not take place at the destruction of Jerusalem.

Proposition VI. The Scriptures teach a universal resurrection of the physically dead—a resurrection unto life of them that have done good, a resurrection unto condemnation of them that have done evil.

We notice, first, the fact of the resurrection of the dead. And proof of this is found in words of Paul mentioned, Acts xxiv:15 : " And have hope toward God, which they themselves also allow, that there shall be a resurrection of the dead, both of the just and unjust." Included in " the dead " are those who were already dead at the time of Paul's speaking; and yet Paul speaks of the resurrection as future. This shows that the resurrection does not take place at the hour of death, but is yet future. And this resurrection is both of the just and the unjust, that is universal.

In Acts xxiii: 6, 8, we learn that Paul was a Pharisee in reference to the doctrine of the resurrection of the dead. " But when Paul perceived that the one part were Sadducees and the other Pharisees, he cried out in the council: ' Men, brethren, I am a Pharisee, the son of a Pharisee, of the hope and resurrection of the dead I am called in question.'"

"The Sadducees say that there is no resurrection, neither angel nor spirit, but the Pharisees confess both."

Josephus, a Jewish priest, who lived in the time of Jerusalem's destruction, speaks thus in a discourse to the Greeks concerning Hades and the resurrection: "This is a discourse concerning Hades, wherein the souls of all men are confined until a proper season, which God hath determined, when he will make a resurrection of all men from the dead, not procuring a transmigration of souls from one body to another, but raising again those very bodies." This opinion Josephus held either as a Jewish priest and Pharisee, or as derived from the early Christians. If as a priest and Pharisee, then the priests and Pharisees believed it; if as derived from the early Christians, then the early Christians believed that the doctrine was taught in their Scriptures.

We now proceed to show that there will be distinctions in the condition of individuals in the resurrection state, according to their conduct in the present life. Paul teaches this in I Thess. iv: 16-18: "The Lord himself shall descend from heaven with a shout, with the voice of the archangel, and with the trump of God; and the dead in Christ shall rise first; then we which are alive and remain shall be caught up together with them in the clouds, to meet the Lord in the air. And so shall we ever be with the Lord. Wherefore comfort one another with these words." Here the "dead in Christ" are believers in Christ who are physically dead at Christ's coming. And "we who are alive and remain unto the coming of the Lord" are believers in Christ who are not physically dead at his coming. For the epistle is directed to the church of the Thessalonians, and the "we" signifies Christians living on the earth at Christ's coming. Both of these classes—the dead preceding the living—are to be caught up to meet the Lord in the air, and to be ever with the Lord. That the resurrection here spoken of is future and does not occur at the hour of death, is evident from the fact that those concerning whom the Thessalonians were sorrowing were already dead at the writing of the epistle, while their resurrection was not to occur until the Lord's descent from heaven, subsequent to the writing of the epistle. They were not to comfort one another because those who slept in Jesus were already resurrected, but because they would be resurrected.

The resurrection change of believers living at the coming of the Lord which in this passage is only implied, is in I Cor. xv: 51, 52, directly asserted: " Behold, I show you a mystery ; we shall not all sleep, but we shall all be changed, in a moment, in the twinkling of an eye, at the last trump: for the trumpet shall sound, and the dead shall be raised incorruptible, and we shall be changed." That this is a change for the better is evident, since Paul in the 57th verse thanks God for it.

That the condition of believers is affected favorably by the resurrection change Paul also teaches in Phil. iii : 20, 21 : " Our conversation is in heaven, from whence also we look for the Saviour, the Lord Jesus Christ, who shall change our vile body, that it may be fashioned like unto his glorious body."

That rewards are experienced in the resurrection, because of good conduct in the present life, Christ teaches, in Luke xiv:12–14: " When thou makest a dinner call not thy friends nor rich neighbors, lest they also bid thee again, and a recompense be made thee; but when thou makest a feast call the poor, the maimed, the lame, the blind ; and thou shalt be blessed; for they cannot recompense thee : for thou shalt be recompensed at the resurrection of the just." That is, do good to them who cannot recompense thee, and thou shalt be recompensed in the resurrection of the just.

What does Christ here mean by "the resurrection of the just"?

By examining the passages in which the word "resurrection" occurs, let us endeavor to ascertain its meaning. Matt. xxii, 23–32: "The same day there came to him the Sadducees who say that there is no resurrection, and asked him, saying, 'Master, Moses said, if a man die having no children, his brother shall marry his wife, and raise up seed unto his brother. Now there were with us seven brethren; and the first, when he had married a wife, deceased. * * * Last of all the woman died also. Therefore, in the resurrection, whose wife shall she be of the seven?'" Here, and in Christ's reply, resurrection must mean life subsequent to physical death. In Mark's account (xii:18, 23), and in Luke's account (xx:27–36), the same word is used, and with the same meaning.

John xi:23,24: "Jesus saith unto her thy brother (dead) shall rise again." Martha saith unto him, "I know that he shall rise again in the resurrection at the last day." Jesus said unto her, "I am the resurrection and the life." Here again, life subsequent to physical death; yet not immediately subsequent, for though four days had passed, the resurrection was still future, and in Martha's estimation would not be until "the last day." Here also a living again of the dead body.

Acts i:22, "Beginning from the baptism of John, unto that same day that he (Christ) was taken up from us, must one be ordained to be a witness with us of his resurrection." Here, a living again of the dead body.

Acts ii:31: "He seeing this before, spake of the resurrection of Christ, that his soul was not left in hell (Hades), neither his flesh did see corruption." Here the reunion of soul and body after physical death.

Acts iv:2: "They taught the people and preached through Jesus the resurrection from the dead." Doubtless a resurrection of the dead body, because it would be patterned after the resurrection of Jesus.

Acts iv:33: "And with great power gave the apostles witness of the resurrection of the Lord Jesus." A resurrection of the dead body.

Acts xvii:18: "He preached unto them Jesus and the resurrection." A living again of the dead body.

Acts xvii:32: "And when they heard of the resurrection of the dead, some mocked." The living again of dead bodies.

Acts xxiii:6: "I am a Pharisee; of the hope and resurrection of the dead I am called in question." The soul after physical death living again in a body.

Acts xxiii:8: "The Sadducees say that there is no resurrection." A living again of the dead body.

Acts xxiv:15: "And have hope toward God, which they themselves also allow, that there shall be a resurrection of the dead, both of the just and the unjust." A living again of the dead body, or the soul after physical death living again in a body.

Acts xxiv:21: "Touching the resurrection of the dead I am called in question." The soul after physical death living again in a body.

Acts xxvi:23: "That Christ should suffer and that he should be the first that should rise from the dead." Here a reunion after physical death of the soul and its body.

Now, in all these instances the word translated "resurrection" means a mode of life, a resurrection subsequent to physical death; and which is, as none will dispute, the final mode of life which the Scriptures reveal.

In the instances given the word is used by Sadducee and Pharisee, by John and Peter and Paul, by Martha and Christ. And omitting the Apocalypse—a highly figurative book—this is the invariable meaning of the word, wherever in the New Testament it is used by Christ or by his apostles.

And therefore the recompense in the resurrection of the just, spoken of by Christ, is the recompense in the final mode of life possessed by the just subsequent to their physical death.

Now, a recompense always and of necessity implies something on account of which the recompense comes. And that thing on account of which this recompense in the resurrection of the just comes, is the giving a feast—the doing good in the earthly life to those unable to make recompense. Very plainly then does Christ teach a connection between good conduct in the earthly life and good condition in the resurrection subsequent to physical death.

That there is a connection between life on earth and condition in the resurrection, is also taught in Heb. xi:35: "Women received their dead raised to life again; and others were tortured, not accepting deliverance, that they might obtain a better resurrection."

This better resurrection cannot be a moral or spiritual one, because those who were tortured, not accepting deliverance, already possessed that. It is the resurrection which faithful believers experience subsequent to physical death; as has already been shown under a previous proposition.

Now, unless these persecuted children of God believed a lie, there is most certainly a connection between conduct in the temporal life and condition in the resurrection life. For they believed that by enduring the torture they would obtain "a better resurrection." But since this was the noble conduct of those who lived by faith, therefore in this particular they did not believe a lie, and therefore there is a connection between good conduct here and good condition hereafter.

Apply also the invariable meaning of "resurrection" as it is used by Christ and his apostles (except in the Apocalypse), and the last clause of the verse will read as follows: "And others were tortured, not accepting deliverance that they might obtain a better 'mode of life' subsequent to physical death." And by this method also we ascertain a connection between conduct here and condition hereafter in the resurrection state.

Now, as these Old Testament worthies, whom the apostle commends for their faith, did not in this important matter labor under a mistake, it therefore follows that had they not endured the torture they would not have obtained "a better resurrection." And of necessary consequence their contemporaries who had no faith, or whose faith died in view of the torture, missed, or will miss the "better resurrection."

And also those who fail to perform those deeds for which men are to be recompensed in the resurrection of the just, will miss the recompense.

In the resurrection, then, there will be distinctions. Some will have the "better resurrection;" some will not. Some will have the "recompense;" some will not.

The fact of a distinction in the resurrection, Christ also teaches with great clearness in John v: 28, 29: "The hour is coming in which all that are in their graves shall hear his voice, and shall come forth; they that have done good, unto the resurrection of life; and they that have done evil, unto the resurrection of damnation."

Apply now to this passage the invariable meaning of the word wherever it is used by Christ, and the passage will read—" All that are in the graves shall hear his voice and shall come forth; they that have done good unto the mode of life, subsequent to physical death, of life; that is—a mode of life which is emphatically life; and they that have done evil unto the mode of life, subsequent to physical death, of condemnation."

Thus, unless our definition of the word as used by Christ be incorrect, there is no escape from the conclusion that Christ teaches a distinction of condition in the resurrection beyond the grave.

To show further the correctness of our definition we will now give the only additional places in which the word is used in the New Testament, omitting the Apocalypse.

Rom. i : 4, "Declared to be the Son of God with power by the resurrection from the dead."

Rom. vi : 5, "If we have been planted in the likeness of his death, we shall be also in the likeness of his resurrection."

Phil. iii :10, "That I may know him (Christ) and the power of his resurrection."

I Pet. i :3, "By the resurrection of Jesus Christ from the dead."

I Pet. iii :21, "By the resurrection of Jesus Christ."

In these places the word plainly relates to the bodily resurrection of Christ.

I Cor. xv:12, 13, "How say some among you that there is no resurrection of the dead; but if there be no resurrection of the dead, then is Christ not risen."

I Cor. xv:21, "Since by man came death, by man came also the resurrection of the dead."

I Cor. xv:42, "So also is the resurrection of the dead."

II Tim. ii:18, "Who concerning the truth have erred, saying that the resurrection is past already."

Heb. vi:2, "Of resurrection of the dead."

Heb. xi:35, "Women received their dead raised to life again;" literally, "received their dead *from* or *through* resurrection."

Now in all these passages, "resurrection" means life subsequent to physical death; and the truth of our definition is necessarily firmly established. And with the correctness of that definition is also established the fact that Christ teaches a distinction of condition in the resurrection beyond the grave. They that have done good, to the resurrection of life; they that have done evil, to the resurrection of condemnation. The only way to escape from such fact is to show that the context does not allow such a meaning. But to show that is impossible.

II. That the resurrection of which Christ here speaks is subsequent to physical death is evident also from the fact that he represents those who are to experience it as being in the graves and to come forth.

"All they that are in the graves shall come forth."

Now the word translated graves is elsewhere translated "tombs" and "sepulchres." It is used about forty times in the New Testament, and in every place apart from this verse, it plainly means the abode of dead bodies; and since there is nothing in the context to forbid that meaning, it also means that here. And therefore it necessarily follows that the resurrection of which Christ speaks is a resurrection subsequent to physical death.

We now give the opinion of some eminent commentators upon the verses. John v: 28, 29): "Few among you now hear my voice aright; but then shall *all* those who have been long in their *graves* (what and wheresoever their graves unknown to man may be), be *compelled* to hear it! And then shall be the final and eternal decision when all *come forth* and are revealed. Then shall there be to believers a judgment also unto life, to unbelievers a new life unto judgment. The unbelievers shall be *awakened*, but not to the life of the Son of God ; *judged*, but not with that merciful judgment of the Son of Man which had been offered in vain before. And then shall there be the *voice* heard—Come forth ! as it was prophetically heard at the grave of Lazarus." Thus Stier in " Words of the Lord Jesus."

" The restoration of life to the body is one day to take place in virtue of the immanent principle of the new life which proceeds from Christ ; this thought is expressed in the form of an image in prevalent use. * * The image which ' the voice ' conveys is expressed in a manner yet more marked by the 'trumpet.'" (1 Cor. xv :52).

" If in zōee (life) there lay simply the idea of duration, the force of krisis, judgment) would be that of annihilation ; as however, zōee ex adjuncta designates that which corresponds with the true idea of life, and consequently, happy life (the *true* life on its subjective side, as it enters into self consciousness) the idea of the krisis (damnation) is that of misery." Thus Tholuck.

" The less is now surpassed by the greater ; yea, even the *universal* resuscitation at the end of time is the work of the Son of God! That the Lord here refers to physical resurrection is shown by the expression en tois mneemeiois (in the graves); as also by ekporeuesthai (come forth), and by the remark that the wicked will rise as well as the good." Thus Olshausen.

In proof of a resurrection unto condemnation we present also Dan. xii:2, " And many of them that sleep in the dust of the earth shall awake; some to everlasting life, and some to shame and everlasting contempt."

First: The Jews previous to the birth of Christ believed in a resurrection subsequent to physical death. This very clearly appears from the words of the heroic martyrs—a mother and her seven sons—as mentioned in II Mac. vii. The mother encouraged them thus—" Doubtless the Creator of the world who formed the generation of man, and found out the beginning of all things, will also of his own mercy give you breath and life again; as ye now regard not yourselves for his law's sake."

The second son spake thus: " Thou like a fury takest us out of the present life, but the King of the world shall raise us up, who have died for his laws, unto everlasting life."

The third: "These (tongue and hands) I had from heaven, and for His laws I despise them, and from Him I hope to receive them again."

The fourth: "It is good being put to death by men to look for hope from God to be raised up again by him; as for thee, thou shalt have no resurrection to life."

The youngest brother: "Our brethren who now have suffered a short pain, are dead under God's covenant of everlasting life."

Second: The Old Testament teaches the doctrine of a resurrection after physical death. For when the Sadducees disputed with Christ against the resurrection he said: "Ye do err not knowing the Scriptures;" *i. e.*, the Scriptures teach the doctrine of the resurrection. And further, "That the dead are raised even Moses showed at the bush, when he called the Lord the God of Abraham, Isaac and Jacob. For he is not a God of the dead but of the living: for all live unto him." (Luke xx:37, 38).

Third: The Jews before Christ and contemporary with Christ believed that the Old Testament taught the doctrine of the resurrection. Witness the words of the martyred mother and her sons 167 years before Christ. Especially where the youngest brother says:

"Our brethren are dead under God's covenant of everlasting life." Witness the agreement of the Scribes with Christ: "Master, thou hast well said." (Luke xx :39).

Fourth: The first reading of the passage conveys to every unprejudiced mind of ordinary intelligence the idea of a resurrection subsequent to physical death. And it would be universally understood to convey such idea, if such idea did not clash with theological opinions which men desire to sustain. And consequently believing Jews who received the plain teaching of God's word, did so understand it.

Fifth: Since the passage suggests universally to unprejudiced minds, the doctrine of a resurrection of the physically dead; since, according to Christ, that doctrine is taught in the Old Testament, and since there is nothing in the context to the contrary, it is therefore a perfectly reasonable conclusion that this passage teaches that doctrine.

Sixth: The interpretation which would confine the event foretold in this passage to the earthly life is necessarily forced to teach that nations in distinction from individuals, are spoken of—that the Jews as a nation are banished for a long, indefinite time from God's favor; that the Gentiles as nations possess that favor through belief in the Gospel. For the moment the passage is applied to individuals as distinct from nations it loses all application to the destruction of Jerusalem and the banishment from gospel privileges of living Jews. For there are at the present time many individual Jews who truly believe in Jesus Christ. And multitudes of Gentiles who reject the reign of Jesus Christ. There are to-day more Gentiles destitute of faith in Christ than there are Jews in the whole world. And there are more unbelieving than believing Gentiles. The passage then, according to the interpretation that would confine its meaning to events of the earthly life, can not be applied, to individuals. But the passage very plainly refers to individuals. "At that time thy people shall be delivered every one that shall be found written in the book." This book is the book of life because those written in it are to awake to everlasting life. In Rev. xx:15 it reads: "Whosoever was not found written in the book of life." These books are the same and therefore individuals are referred to. And consequently the passage does not relate to the destruction of Jerusalem and the exclusion of the Jewish nation from the church on earth. That individuals are referred to appears also from the passage itself—"And many of them that sleep in the dust of the earth shall awake, some to everlasting life, and some to shame and everlasting contempt." Here some means some of them that sleep. Applied to individuals in the final resurrection, all is plain and true. But where are the nations which in the earthly life awake to shame and everlasting contempt?

Seventh: The fact that Daniel should rest and stand in his lot, at the end of the days, shows that the event referred to is not the destruction of Jerusalem.

For on either interpretation, the death of Daniel occurred long before the fulfilment of the prophecy. And since the sentence, "Thou shalt rest and stand in thy lot," is not applicable to a man considered simply as about to die, but is very appropriately applied to one who is both to die, and also to experience a blessed resurrection, therefore the prophecy was not fulfilled at the destruction of Jerusalem. For at the end of the days—that is—the time of the prophecy's fulfilment, Daniel shall be raised from the dead; and he was not so raised at the destruction of Jerusalem.

Eighth: "And they that be wise shall shine as the brightness of the firmament; and they that turn many to righteousness as the stars forever and ever."

This verse immediately follows the one under consideration, and is doubtless to be fulfilled at the same time. And it is certainly nonsense to confine such a glorious promise of God as this to the brief and very imperfect life of the Christian on earth.

Proposition VII. The Scriptures do not teach that the condemnation experienced by the wicked in the judgment subsequent to the final or general resurrection will ever be removed; nor that the painful results of that condemnation will ever cease; in other words, they do not teach a universal restoration of lost men to the favor of God.

We now proceed to notice the principal passages which are presented as proofs of a universal restoration.

Luke xx:36: "They are equal unto the angels, and are the children of God, being the children of the resurrection."

From this passage it is inferred that all who are raised from the dead are raised to a state of holiness and happiness; and since all are to be raised from the 'dead, therefore all are to be holy and happy. Here the point to be determined is—whether the resurrection spoken of is to be experienced by the entire race of man? And unless the affirmative of this question can be, not asserted, but proved, the passage contains no argument for universal salvation.

The following facts make the affirmation of this question impossible to be proved:

1. The words of Christ in the previous verse clearly imply that those who shall obtain the resurrection spoken of, must previously " be accounted worthy to obtain" it. He says, "They who shall be accounted worthy to obtain" "the resurrection." Should a king say, " Those soldiers who shall be accounted worthy of extra pay at the expiration of their term of service, shall be generously cared for through life, what soldier in all the army so dull as not to understand that a certain standard of worthiness *must* be attained before the favors spoken of can be enjoyed? Will Universalists affirm that in the case supposed, the extra pay, and the generous care through life, are affirmed in behalf of all the soldiers—be they cowards, deserters or traitors? We trow not. But if not, then by what authority do they affirm that Christ,

when he speaks of those "who shall be accounted worthy to obtain that world and the resurrection," means the entire race of man? Has not prejudice warped the judgment?

2. In each of the three other passages in the New Testament, where the word translated "to account worthy" is used, a standard of worthiness is plainly implied; and said standard is or was actually attained unto by but a portion of mankind. Luke xxi:36, "Watch ye therefore and pray always that ye may be accounted worthy to escape all these things that shall come to pass, and to stand before the Son of man."

Both Universalist and Orthodox understand that those in this passage counted worthy to escape, include but a portion of mankind, and that the said portion attained or will attain to the standard of worthiness.

Acts v:41: "They departed from the presence of the council rejoicing that they were counted worthy to suffer shame for his name."

Here the being counted worthy is limited to the disciples of Jesus; and those who have not become disciples have not attained the standard of worthiness. For certainly, in the sense in which the words are here used, none but disciples suffer shame for his name.

II Thess. i:4, 5 : "Your persecutions and tribulations that ye endure—a manifest token of the righteous judgment of God that ye may be counted worthy of the kingdom of God for which ye also suffer." Here also a standard of worthiness is implied, and to this standard but a portion of mankind attain. For whether the kingdom of God be considered as then existing, or as to exist at Christ's second coming, it includes but a portion of mankind. For as then existing it did not include the persecutors; and as to exist at Christ's coming it will not include those "who shall be punished with everlasting destruction from the presence of the Lord" (v. 9.) Now from the fact that a standard of worthiness is implied in every passage, apart from that in dispute where the word is used, it is perfectly reasonable to conclude, there being nothing in the context to the contrary, that a standard of worthiness is also implied n the disputed passage.

3. Paul conclusively teaches in Phil. iii:8–11 that a standard of worthiness must be attained before one can attain unto the resurrection of the dead. He suffered the loss of all things that he might win Christ and be found in him, and know Christ and the power of his resurrection and the fellowship of his

sufferings, being made conformable unto his death, if by any means he might attain unto the resurrection of the dead. When one suffers the loss of all things to gain a certain object it is conclusive proof of his belief that the gaining of the object is conditional on the sacrifices that he makes—that the object can not be gained independent of his own effort. What pearl diver would brave the ocean depths would the pearls come to him without his diving? What gold miner would undergo the toil of mining, would the gold come without the toil? . What man of sound mind would suffer the loss of all things to attain an object certain to be attained without any loss? Universalists will hardly assert that Paul was crazy, or a fanatic. Yet, if all men without exception and independent of their own effort are to attain unto the resurrection of the dead, Paul was nothing less than a fanatic, for he suffered the loss of all things to gain that which he would certainly gain though he suffered no loss. The conclusion cannot be escaped from that either Paul was a fanatic, or Universalism is false. But Paul was not a fanatic. He says (II Tim. i:7): "God hath not given us the spirit of fear; but of power, and of love, and of a sound mind."

4. The Scriptural usage of the word children does not justify the conclusion that because all men are to be raised from the dead, therefore, all men are to be "children of the resurrection," in the sense in which Christ uses the phrase.

In one sense all men are children of the "Father which is in heaven," yet not in the sense in which Christ uses the phrase. For he says (Matt. v:44, 45): "Love your enemies, bless them that curse you, do good to them that hate you, and pray for them which despitefully use you, and persecute you; that ye may be the children of your Father which is in heaven." Here Christ plainly teaches that a special course of conduct is necessary that we may be "children" of the Heavenly Father. Of course, then, those who have not that conduct are not in Christ's sense "children" of the Father.

Christ also told the Jews who claimed God as their Father: "If God were your father, ye would love me." "Ye are of your father the devil." (John. viii:42, 44.)

In one sense all men are "children of this world," yet not in the sense in which Christ uses the phrase. For he says (Luke xvi:8): "The children of this world are in their generation wiser than the children of light."

These two classes are composed of different persons, else the one class could not be wiser than the other. The children of light are those who believe in Jesus. For he says, (John xii:36): "While ye have the light believe in the light, that ye may be children of light." And (v. 46): "I am come a light into the world that whosoever believeth on me should not abide in darkness." And therefore the children of this world are, not all men, but those who refuse to believe in Jesus.

In one sense all descendants of Abraham are "children of Abraham," yet not in the sense in which Christ uses the word "children." For to the Jews who claimed Abraham as their father he said (John, viii:39, 40): "If ye were Abraham's children ye would do the works of Abraham. But now ye seek to kill me, a man that hath told you the truth, which I have heard of God. This did not Abraham." Not doing the works of Abraham, they were not, in Christ's sense, children of Abraham. Paul also says (Rom. ix:6, 7): "They are not all Israel which are of Israel. Neither because they are the seed of Abraham are they all children."

Now since creation and preservation by the Heavenly Father does not make men necessarily "children" of the Father, since living in this world does not make men, necessarily, "children of this world," since being descendants of Abraham does not necessarily make men "children of Abraham," therefore, in like manner, the being raised from the dead does not necessarily make men "children of the resurrection." But if not, then the fact that the "children of the resurrection" are to be holy and blessed, does not prove that all men, without exception, are to be holy and blessed.

5. At the time the Sadducees questioned Jesus, the law of Moses was still in force, and was to Sadducee and Pharisee the law of God. Those, therefore, who obeyed that law, were considered by them, and should be considered by us, as righteous persons. But the seven brethren and the wife are represented as obedient to the law of Moses, which was the law of God, and consequently they are to be regarded as righteous persons. And therefore the real question which the Sadducees asked the Saviour, is: In the resurrection of these righteous persons—the seven brethren and one wife—whose wife of the seven is she? for the seven had her to wife.

And since the question was concerning the condition of the righteous in the resurrection, therefore the reply also was concerning the condition of the righteous in the resurrection. But how the blessedness in the resurrection state of those who have lived righteously, proves that there is blessedness in the resurrection state for those who have lived in wickedness and died in impenitence, we confess ourselves utterly unable to see.

6. The objection of the Sadducees has force only on the supposition that the marriage institution exists in the resurrection state. "Whose wife of them is she?" Now, should we suppose with the Sadducee that if the resurrection be a fact, marriage is connected with it, against what kind of a resurrection would the marriage institution be an objection? A happy, or an unhappy one? Very plainly not an unhappy one, since the unhappiness which would result from marriage under such circumstances, is the very point of the objection made against the resurrection. Against the doctrine of a happy resurrection, then, was the objection of the Sadducees urged. They seem to have thought that a happy resurrection was the strong defence of the whole resurrection system, and, *that* once overthrown, the whole system would fall of itself. And therefore, since the attack falls on the doctrine of a

happy resurrection, Christ defends that doctrine with the unanswerable reply, "They which shall be accounted worthy to obtain that world and the resurrection from the dead, neither marry, nor are given in marriage." But between the doctrine of a happy resurrection, which Christ defends, and the doctrine that all men without exception will experience that resurrection, there is no necessary connection.

7. Both in the question of the Sadducees and in the reply of Jesus, the word translated resurrection has prefixed to it the definite article. This shows that a special resurrection is meant. Should one say, "The star is hidden by a cloud," or "The lamp is brightly shining," a special star, or lamp, would be meant. So when the Sadducees and Jesus speak of "the resurrection," they mean a special resurrection. Now, the Jews of that day believed in but one kind of resurrection as to occur subsequent to physical death, or they believed in more kinds than one as thus to occur. If in but one kind, then most certainly Jesus is speaking of a blessed resurrection; and all will admit that such as experience that, are children of God, and blessed. But if in more kinds than one, then "the resurrection" signifies that kind of a resurrec-

tion which believing and righteous Jews most prized and themselves hoped to obtain; that which was to them emphatically "the resurrection;" and most certainly that kind of a resurrection was a resurrection of blessedness. But from Christ's affirmation that they who shall obtain a blessed resurrection, are children of God, it does not follow that all men without exception are children of God.

In reference to the teachings of Christ the following admission has been made by a talented advocate of final restoration, the Rev. T. S. King: "And yet I freely say that I do not find the doctrine of the ultimate salvation of all souls clearly stated in any text, or in any discourse that has ever been reported from the lips of Christ. I do not think that we can fairly maintain that the final restoration of all men is a prominent and explicit doctrine of the four gospels." (Two Discourses, p. 5.)

Theodore Parker, also an advocate of universal salvation, has made the following statement: "*To me it is quite clear that Jesus taught the doctrine of eternal damnation*, if the Evangelists—the first three, I mean—are to be treated as inspired. I can understand his language in no other way."

Acts iii:21: "Whom the heaven must receive until the times of restitution of all things, which God hath spoken by the mouth of all his holy prophets since the world began." Here the "all things" are confined to the things which God has spoken by the Old Testament prophets. And so long as advocates of universal salvation deny that the prophets of the Old Testament teach the doctrine of man's immortality, it seems reasonable that they should feel themselves restrained from presenting such a passage as the above as proof of a happy immortality for all mankind. For, certainly, if the said prophets do not teach man's immortality, they do not teach his happy and universal immortality. Yet, passing by the argumentum ad hominem, the passage is no proof of universal salvation; since no single one of the Old Testament prophets, much less all, predicted the final salvation of all mankind. In immediate connection with the mention of "restitution of all things" the apostle presents the prediction of one of said prophets, Moses, who says (v. 23), "It shall come to pass that every soul which will not hear that Prophet (Jesus) shall be destroyed from among the people." This destruction from among the people is penalty for disobedience and unbelief. But this penalty as was proved under the previous proposition, is condemnation in the resurrection subsequent to physical death. And therefore, unless there can be proved a restoration from that condemnation, the above passage is no proof of the final salvation of all mankind. But to prove such a restoration is impossible. And so long as it is impossible to prove by Old Testament prophecies the happy immortality of universal mankind, so long will the above passage fail as a proof text of universal salvation. But when such an immortality can be proved by said prophecies, Universalists will no longer need the above passage as a proof text. One of the Old Testament prophets says of Jesus (Ps. ii:9,12): "Thou shalt break them with a rod of iron; thou shalt dash them in pieces like a potter's vessel." "Kiss the Son lest he be angry, and ye perish from the way when his wrath is kindled but a little." This does not seem like a prediction of universal restoration. Another says (Mal. iv:1), "The day cometh that shall burn as an oven, and all the proud, yea, and all that do wickedly, shall be stubble; and the day that cometh, shall burn them up, saith the Lord of Hosts, that it shall leave them neither root nor branch." It is certainly difficult to see that Malachi teaches universal restoration.

Christ throws light on the meaning of "restitution of all things" in his reply to his disciples, Matt. xvii:11, "Elias truly shall first come and restore all things." Now, to "restore all things" means, in other words, to accomplish the restoration of all things. And if to accomplish the restoration of all things does not mean the final salvation of all men, neither does the restitution of all things mean such salvation. For restitution is no stronger in meaning than restoration. Now, since the restoration of all things spoken of as to be effected by Elias, means simply the work wrought by John the Baptist (v. 13), and since that work did not save all men, therefore the restitution of all things does not mean the salvation of all men. It simply means the "full establishment" of the Messiah's kingdom, and that kingdom may be fully established, even though its enemies are lost.

Rom. xiv:11: "For it is written, 'As I live, saith the Lord, every knee shall bow to me, and every tongue shall confess to God.'" It is strange that this passage should be offered as proof of universal salvation by any one who has read the verses immediately preceding and following. The verses clearly show that this passage is introduced as proof of a universal judgment. "But why dost thou judge thy brother? or why dost thou set at nought thy brother? for we shall all stand at the judgment seat of Christ." Then as proof of so standing, comes the 11th verse: "For it is written, 'As I live, saith the Lord, every knee shall bow to me, and every tongue shall confess to God." And then further, as an inference from this proof, comes the 12th verse, "So then every one of us shall give account of himself to God." But in what way the fact of a universal judgment proves a universal salvation, puzzles any one but a Universalist to see. The sentiment certainly seems anti-Scriptural; for in the universal judgment mentioned in Matt. xxv: 31-46, the King says to them on the left hand, "Depart from me, ye cursed, into everlasting fire."

But should it be said that the passage in Isaiah to which Paul refers teaches that every one who confesses to God is to possess in the Lord righteousness and strength, we reply that such a view of that passage is an erroneous one. It teaches that every tongue or person shall confess to God, but does not teach that every person thus confessing, shall say, " In the Lord have I righteousness and strength." Isa. xlv:23, 24 is the passage referred to, and translating the 24th verse rather more strictly than is done in the English version, is as follows (v. 23) : " I have sworn by myself, the word is gone out of my mouth in righteousness and shall not return. That unto me every knee shall bow, every tongue shall swear." (v. 24): "Surely to me every tongue shall say, In the Lord are righteousness and strength. Unto him all that are incensed against him shall come and shall be ashamed."

To help make the correctness of this translation evident to the reader not versed in Hebrew, we give a literal translation of the words of the 24th verse in the order in which they occur :

"Surely — In the Lord, to me [every tongue] shall say, righteousnesses [are] and strength. Unto him shall come and shall be ashamed all that are incensed with him."

The correctness of this translation of the separate words of the verse (together with the insertion of the words in brackets so far as they bear on the question at issue) we presume no Restorationist able to read Hebrew will dispute. Taking this for granted, the point to be determined is, whether the words "to me" qualify " shall say," or qualify "righteousnesses and strength." If the former, the verse reads thus : "Surely every tongue shall say to me, In the Lord are righteounesses and strength." If the latter, it then reads: "Surely every tongue shall say, In the Lord righteousnesses and strength are to me."

That these qualify "shall say" the following reasons furnish sufficient evidence:

1. In the original, the words "to me" join "shall say," while they are more distant from "righteousnesses and strength."

2. It is a fact, as the 23d verse teaches, that all knees must bow and tongues must swear to God. Now it is in perfect harmony with this fact that "to me" is made to qualify "shall say," thus: "Unto me every knee shall bow, and tongue shall swear—surely shall say to me," etc.

This bowing of the knee and swearing of the tongue is plainly more indicative of the authority of God than of the faith and righteousness of man.

3. To join "shall say" and "to me" is in perfect and plain harmony with Paul's understanding of the passage as given in Rom. xiv:11, 12, thus: "For it is written, As I live, saith the Lord, every knee shall bow to me, and every tongue shall confess to God. So then every one of us shall give account of himself to God."

Paul here uses the passage as a warning,

and not as a proof of security. But to connect the " to me" with "righteousness and strength" makes the passage not a warning, but a proof of security.

4. The context forbids that the passage be so understood as to favor universal salvation.

Verse 17 says of Israel, "Ye shall not be ashamed nor confounded world without end."

But our verse (24) says, " All that are incensed against him shall be ashamed."

5. The simplicity and frequency of the grammatical construction in the one case, and the complexity and infrequency in the other.

I Cor. xv:55. " O death, where is thy sting? O grave, where is thy victory?"

The word here rendered "grave" is in the original Greek, " Hades." And the inquiry arises as to what Paul means by " Hades." And to obtain a correct answer to the inquiry, let us notice first, the context; second, other passages where the word occurs.

In the previous context Paul asserts three principal facts: First, the resurrection of Christ—" He rose again the third day according to the Scriptures," (v. 4); second, the sure resurrection of the dead—" If there be no resurrection of the dead, then is Christ not risen," (v. 13); third, the transformation of believers who shall be alive at the sounding of the last trumpet. (vs. 51, 52): "We shall not all sleep, but we shall all be changed, in a moment, in the twinkling of an eye, at the last trump."

Then, after affirming the necessity of this glorious change, and stating that it occurs in accordance with a specific prediction, he utters the triumphant language of our passage: "O death, where is thy sting? O Hades, where is thy victory?" The subject then on which the apostle is discoursing is, the triumph of dead and dying men over Death and Hades. Now, since these men are to triumph over Hades, Hades must, of course, be considered as in antagonism to them. But since, as all parties affirm, the apostle himself and those who sleep in Jesus, and the beloved brethren whom Paul exhorted to always abound in the work of the Lord, and the holiest of Christians, are included among these dead and dying men; and since it is strongly anti-scriptural, if not blasphemous, to assert that the holiest of Christians must undergo positive punishment in Hades, therefore Hades must be understood here, not as a place where departed spirits suffer punishment, but as a place where dwell, until the resurrection, the departed souls of those who sleep in Jesus. And when that resurrection takes place, then these souls and all Christians triumph over Death and Hades. And since not a hint is given in the whole chapter (we elsewhere explain v. 22) that the wicked are to experience the blessed resurrection of which this chapter treats; and since it is asserted (v. 58) that the labor of Christians is not in vain, which must be in vain if the wicked experience the same triumph, therefore the defeat of Hades by the triumphant resurrection of all Christians, is no proof of universal salvation.

The ten other passages of the New Testament in which Hades occurs, are as follows:

Matt. xi:23, and Luke x:15 : " And thou Capernaum, which art exalted unto heaven, shalt be brought down to hell (Hades)." In both these places used not in a literal but a figurative sense, since in contrast with a figurative heaven.

Matt. xvi:18 : " Upon this rock I will build my church, and the gates of hell (Hades) shall not prevail against it." Here the " gates of Hades " signify the powers of the unseen world, which are considered as antagonistic to Christ's church, because they attempt to hold the people of Christ in subjection.

Luke xvi:23 : " And in hell (Hades) he lifted up his eyes, being in torments." He was, indeed, in torment in Hades. But this does not prove that all souls in Hades were in torment, any more than the fact that some persons were drowned in a certain river, proves that all persons who were in that river were drowned.

Acts ii:27, 31 : " Thou wilt not leave my soul in hell (Hades)." " His soul was not left in hell (Hades)." Spoken of the soul of Christ, and therefore meaning simply the world of the dead, since Christ experienced no suffering after his physical death.

Rev. i:18 : " I am alive for evermore, Amen; and have the keys of hell (Hades) and death."

Rev. vi:8 : " And I looked and behold a pale horse; and his name that sat on him was Death, and hell (Hades) followed with him."

Rev. xx:13 : " And death and hell (Hades) delivered up the dead which were in them."

Rev. xx:14 : " And death and hell (Hades) were cast into the lake of fire." Probably in all these places used to signify the unseen abode of disembodied spirits. Thus it is seen both from the context and the general signification of Hades in the New Testament that there is no necessary connection between the total defeat of Hades and universal salvation.

Rom. viii:19–23 : " For the earnest expectation of the creature waiteth for the manifestation of the sons of God. For the creature was made subject to vanity, not willingly, but by reason of him who hath subjected the same in hope, because the creature itself also shall be delivered into the glorious liberty of the children of God. For we know that the whole creation groaneth and travaileth in pain together, until now. And not only they but ourselves also, which have the first fruits of the Spirit, even we ourselves groan within ourselves, waiting for the adoption, to wit, the redemption of the body."

The deliverance referred to in the 21st verse is doubtless actual and complete. And therefore the force of the passage as an argument for universal salvation depends on the meaning of the word translated "creature" in the same verse. If that word as there used includes of necessity in its meaning the entire human race or that entire part of the race which lives and dies without faith in Christ, then the passage presents a powerful argument for universal salvation. But if the word as there used necessarily includes in its meaning, neither the entire human race, nor that entire portion of it which lives and dies without faith in Christ, then the passage furnishes no proof of universal salvation.

That the word as there used does not include in its meaning the entire race is evident from the fact that in the 23d verse the apostle plainly distinguishes between believers in Christ who have received the "first fruits of the Spirit," and "the creature," or "the whole creation." For he says: "And not only the creature, or the whole creation, but ourselves also which have the first fruits of the Spirit, even we, ourselves, do groan within ourselves, waiting for the adoption, the redemption of the body." This distinction is so plain that none need overlook it.

2. The undeniable fact that the sacred writers represent inanimate creation as possessing the feelings of rational beings, excludes all necessity for including in the meaning of "creature" the persistently wicked.

The prophet Jeremiah says (xii:4): "How long shall the land mourn, and the herbs of every field wither, for the wickedness of them that dwell therein."

Isaiah says (xxiv:4,5): "The earth mourneth and fadeth away, the world languisheth, the haughty people of the earth do languish. The earth also is defiled under the inhabitants thereof, because they have transgressed the laws."

Here each prophet represents the land or

earth as experiencing suffering because of the wickedness of the inhabitants. Now, it surely is just as appropriate for Paul to represent the inanimate creation as expecting deliverance from woe in common with the sons of God, as for the prophets to represent the earth as experiencing calamity in common with wicked men. Since it not willingly shared in the curse through Adam (Gen. iii: 17), let it willingly share in the blessing through Christ.

But the sacred writers go still further than we have quoted. And this very same principle of joyful sympathy which Paul represents as existing between the children of God and the inanimate creation, they also represent as existing between the people of God and the inanimate creation.

Isaiah says (xlix:13): " Sing, O heavens, and be joyful, O earth, and break forth into singing, O mountains ; for the Lord hath comforted his people, and will have mercy upon his afflicted."

The Psalmist says (xcviii:8,9): "Let the floods clap their hands; let the hills be joyful together before the Lord, for he cometh to judge the earth; with righteousness shall he judge the world, and the people with equity." These passages of Scripture do plainly show that there is no necessity whatever for including in the meaning of "creature" (as in Rom. viii:21) those who live and die rejecting Christ.

3. In the writings of Josephus, the Jewish historian, who was contemporaneous with Paul, there occurs a passage which shows, not only that there is no necessity for including the unbelieving in the "creature" or creation spoken of, but also that, without positive proof to that effect, it is really improper to include them. In his "Discourse to the Greeks concerning Hades" Josephus* speaks as follows: "For all men, the just as well as the unjust, shall be brought before God, the word; for to him hath the Father committed all judgment; and he, in order to fulfil the will of his Father, shall come as Judge, whom we call Christ. For Minos and Radamanthus are not the judges as you Greeks do suppose, but he whom God, even the Father, hath glorified; concerning whom we have elsewhere given a more particular account for the sake of those who seek after truth. This person, exercising the righteous judgment of the Father toward all men, hath prepared a just sentence for every one according to his works; at whose judgment seat, when all

---

*Whiston's translation.

men and angels and demons shall stand, they will send forth one voice and say, Just is thy judgment; the rejoinder to which will bring a just sentence upon both parties, by giving justly to those that have done well an everlasting fruition; but allotting to the lovers of wicked works eternal punishment. To these belong the unquenchable fire, and that without end, and a certain fiery worm never dying, and not destroying the body, but continuing its eruption out of the body with never ceasing grief; neither will sleep give ease to these men, nor will the night afford them comfort; death will not free them from their punishment, nor will the interceding prayers of their kindred profit them; for the just are no longer seen by them, nor are they thought worthy of remembrance; but the just shall remember only their righteous actions whereby they have attained the heavenly kingdom, in which there is no sleep, no sorrow, no corruption, no care, no night, no day measured by time, no sun driven in his course along the circle of heaven by necessity, and measuring out the bounds and conversions of the seasons, for the better illumination of the light of men; no moon decreasing or increasing, or introducing a variety of seasons, nor will she then moisten the earth; no burning sun, no bear turning round (the pole), no Orion to rise, no wandering of innumerable stars. The earth then will not be difficult to be passed over, nor will it be hard to find out the court of Paradise, nor will there be any fearful roaring of the sea, forbidding the passengers to walk on it; even that will be made easily passable to the just, though it will not be void of moisture. Heaven will not then be uninhabitable by men, and it will not be impossible to discover the way of ascending thither. The earth will not then be uncultivated, nor require too much labor of men, but will bring forth its fruits of its own accord, and will be well adorned with them. The number of the righteous will continue, and never fail, together with righteous angels and spirits (of God), and with his word, as a choir of righteous men and women that never grow old, and continue in an incorruptible state, singing hymns to God who hath advanced them to that happiness by the means of a regular institution of life; with whom the *whole creation* also will lift up a perpetual hymn from corruption to incorruption, as glorified by a splendid and pure spirit. It will not then be restrained by a bond of necessity, but with a lively freedom shall offer up a voluntary hymn, and shall praise him that made them, together with the angels and spirits and men now freed from all bondage." If Josephus, while believing in endless punishment can yet speak of "the whole creation" lifting up "a perpetual hymn from corruption into incorruption," surely Paul, while believing in endless punishment, may be allowed to say: "The creature itself shall also be delivered from the bondage of corruption into the glorious liberty of the children of God."

4. The immediate context forbids the idea that the persistently wicked are included in the "creature" spoken of in the 21st verse. For the "creature" in v. 21 is the very same as in v. 19. But in the "creature" of v. 19 the wicked in heart cannot be included. For neither in figurative nor literal statement can it be truthfully said, "that the earnest expectation of the wicked waiteth for the manifestation of the sons of God." This manifestation doubtless brings on God's children glorious blessings. Now since the unbelieving and wicked either have no faith in those blessings, or lack that regard for God's people which would cause them to wait with earnest expectation for blessings on them, the wicked must necessarily be excluded from the meaning of "creature" as used in the 21st verse.

Rom. v:18: "So then, as through one trespass the judgment came unto all men to condemnation, even so through one act of righteousness the free gift came unto all men to justification of life." (Rev. Ver.)

Here the question for decision is: Must the all men justified be the very same in persons and in number as the all men condemned? Or, may the persons justified be less in number than the persons condemned? The one trespass is Adam's. The one righteousness is Christ's. In verse 14 Paul says that Adam is a figure or type of him that was to come. There is, then, a resemblance between the Adam and the Christ. This resemblance cannot be in their moral character, for the one was a transgressor, the other was sinless. Through transgression is condemnation, through righteousness is justification. Through Adam's transgression is condemnation. Through Christ's righteousness is justification. *As* through Adam's transgression there is condemnation to all men, *so* through Christ's righteousness there is justification to all men. How, through Adam's sin, is there condemnation to all men? Because of some relation existing between Adam and all men. Adam is the human father, the all men are his children. They share his character. They stand or fall through him. In his standing they stand, in his falling they fall. He stands for them. All men that he stands for share, through his moral act, his condition. Do any more men? *No.* Then, through Adam's act of transgression, all his children—all his family—were condemned. This is in accordance with what the Scriptures teach concerning Adam after his transgression. " And Adam begat a son in his own likeness, after his image." (Gen. v:3.) And, also, no more men than were his family were condemned through his transgression. In the first part of the comparison the all men relate to Adam, and are his family. Just so, in the latter part of the comparison, the all men relate to Christ, and are his family.

Thus: *As* Adam and his family.

So Christ and his family.

The comparison is between Adam and his influence over his entire family, and Christ and his influence over his entire family. Adam and Christ are two heads of families. Inserting now these ideas into the comparison, we have:

As through Adam's transgression all Adam's family were condemned, *so* through Christ's righteousness all Christ's family shall be justified.

But who are Christ's family? As Adam's family are those who follow him in line of natural descent, and partake of his nature and are unregenerate, so Christ's family are those who follow him in line of spiritual descent and partake of his nature, and are regenerate—are spirit-born. As the Scripture elsewhere says: If any man have not the Spirit of Christ, he is none of his; and, Ye must be born again. The family of Christ, then, are the regenerate. Putting this idea into the comparison, we have: As through Adam's transgression all his family were condemned, so through Christ's righteousness all the regenerate shall be justified. This is the meaning of the verse. And since there is nothing here that teaches that, sooner or later, all the children of Adam shall become regenerate, therefore the verse affords no proof of mankind's universal justification. This manner of understanding the verse is in exact harmony with what Paul teaches in the context. He says, in verse 17: They that receive the abundance of grace and of the gift of righteousness shall reign in life through Jesus Christ. It is also in exact harmony with what Jesus teaches in Matt. vii:23: "I never knew you, depart from me, ye that work iniquity."

We are inclined to think that some who accept the Bible as the word of God have been misled as to the true teaching of this verse, because they have not correctly understood the influence of the two words "as" and "so."

By virtue of these two words, that principle that ties the first "all men" to Adam and limits them to Adam's family; that same principle ties the second "all men" to Christ, and limits them to Christ's family.

In order to bring out, if possible, the meaning of the verse yet more clearly, we mention the following parallel statement by way of illustration :

As by the unwise management of Dr. A, all the inmates of the hospital suffered loss, so by the wise management of Dr. B, all the inmates of the hospital experienced benefit.

This sentence in the manner of its construction is a perfect parallel to the verse which is under consideration. The "as" and "so" are similarly placed, and exert similar influence. And the number in each part of the comparison is "all."

In this parallel sentence the first "all" signifies all the inmates under Dr. A's management; and the second "all" signifies all the inmates under Dr. B's management. But the management of the one was subsequent to the management of the other; and the number of the inmates of the hospital was constantly changing. Under Dr. B, there may have been, for anything the sentence says to the contrary, twice the number that there was under Dr. A. And also for anything the sentence says to the contrary, there may have been under Dr. B's management but one-half of the other number. And just as in this sentence, which, so far as reasoning from the one sentence to the other is concerned, is a perfect parallel to that in Rom. v:18, the two "alls" are not bound together into equality of number, so also in Rom. v: 18 the two "alls" are not bound together into equality of number.

Permit the mentioning of another parallel.

As by Gen. McDowell's defeat at Bull Run all Union soldiers were depressed, so by Gen. Grant's victory at Petersburg, all Union soldiers were encouraged.

This comparison is of a like construction to the one in Rom. v:18. Each member of the comparison has all Union soldiers, just as each member of the comparison in Rom. v:18 has "all men."

But the number of soldiers comprised in

the phrase "all Union soldiers" in the first member of the comparison, is very different from the number comprised in the phrase " all Union soldiers" in the second member of the comparison. The "all Union soldiers" first spoken of were probably less than two hundred thousand men ; and the "all Union solders" next spoken of were probably nearly a million of men. And notwithstanding everything the comparison says, the two numbers might be reversed. That is to say, the comparison would be just as correct and appropriate if there had been one million Union soldiers in the time of Gen. McDowell's defeat, and but two hundred thousand Union soldiers in the time of Gen. Grant's victory. And thus there is nothing in the sentence that compels the one multitude of "all Union soldiers" to equal in number the other multitude of "all Union soldiers."

And since the sentence we are considering is a fair parallel in construction to Rom. v:18, therefore there is nothing in Rom. v:18 that compels the one multitude of "all men" to equal in number the other multitude of "all men."

It seems that the Bible nowhere states the exact proportion between the numbers of the saved and the lost. And the Christ when asked, "Lord, are there few that be saved?" replied, "Strive to enter in at the strait gate; for many, I say unto you, will seek to enter in and shall not be able;" and gave no insight into the comparative numbers of the lost and the saved.

Influenced by the teaching of other parts of Scripture we believe that Paul in the last "all men" of Rom. v:18, meant not "all" of Adam's race, but only "some" of Adam's race. If so, why then did not Paul say "some men"?

Because of the relation which the second "men" in the sentence sustains to Christ. The flow of thought is as follows: *As*, Adam —sin of Adam—condemnation of Adam and *all* his natural descendants; *So*, Christ— righteousness of Christ—justification of Christ and *all* his spiritual descendants.

Shall Christ be justified and not *all* his spiritual family? No, indeed. As Adam brings into condemnation all his, so Christ brings into justification all his.

And so Paul must say "all" in order to affirm that no single one of Christ's family shall be condemned; but that every one of Christ's family shall be justified.

And thus he affirms, as the "so" requires, that Christ's influence is as universal over his family, as Adam's influence is over his family. The totality of the saved are saved by the Christ. There is no other Saviour. " There is none other name under heaven given among men, whereby we must be saved." "We are shut up unto the faith." " As many as received him, to them gave he power to become the sons of God, even to them that believe on his name; which were born not of blood, nor of the will of the flesh, nor of the will of man, but of God."

Receive this divine physician, actually apply to him for the healing which he bestows, and you will be justified and saved.

That the children of Adam should have a being and character like his, should not be thought an unfair thing. It is in accordance with the act of God in his constitution of all living, earthly things. Man, beast, bird, insect, reptile, tree, plant, flower, all produce according to their kind. "Men do not gather grapes of thorns, nor figs of thistles. " And the earth brought forth grass and herb yielding seed after his kind, and the tree yielding fruit whose seed was in itself after his kind. And God saw that it was good." (Gen. i:12.) " And God made the beast of the earth after his kind, and cattle after their kind, and everything that creepeth upon the earth after his kind, and God saw that it was good." (Gen. i:25.)

"There is *one* kind of flesh of men, *another* flesh of beasts, another of fishes, and another of birds." (I Cor. xv:39.) Neither the Bible nor natural science knows anything of that sort of evolution in nature which makes the offspring different in kind from the parent. From bird, bird; from beast, beast; from wheat, wheat; from man, man. Any other law would cut up the very roots of human knowledge, and in all likelihood destroy man from the earth. How much better God's law! The living creature after his kind, which God saw was good. This law in a thousand forms has wrought good for humanity ever since the first man's creation. But shall we receive good at the hands of the Lord, and not receive evil? (Job ii:10.) If the law be good shall man complain when by his fault the law works against him? Had man remained in goodness, he would have had perpetual favor. In this he would have greatly rejoiced. Through transgression he lost favor. He should still say with Paul — The law is holy, just, and good. (Rom. vii: 12.) And with Paul he should seek refuge in him who is the wisdom of God, and the power of God unto salvation.

The position which Christ occupies, suggests a miracle. If he were simply an ordinary descendant of Adam, would he not, like all ordinary descendants, be himself a transgressor? "As in Adam all die"—obtain a dying and fallen nature, become personal transgressors, and experience condemnation. But the Christ had no fallen nature, and no personal transgressions. And apart from violence we think the holy body of the Christ would never have died.

But however that may be, he was "separate from sinners." (Heb. vii:26.) He "was tempted in all points, like as we are, yet without sin." A personal sin would have made it impossible for him to be a fountain of spiritual life—to be, as the apostle indicates, the anti-type to Adam. He would, then, have been but a part of universally fallen humanity, deriving their origin from Adam. But, on the contrary, he stands in contrast to Adam. Adam transgresses and dies. Christ obeys and lives; lives with "the power of endless life." (Heb. vii:16.)

There *must* be a new power at work. The Christ *cannot* be of the natural posterity of Adam. Adam was a miraculous formation. So was the Christ, but of a higher order. And so we read as the message of an angel to a virgin, blessed and highly favored: " The Holy Ghost shall come upon thee, and the power of the Highest shall overshadow thee; therefore also that holy thing which shall be born of thee, shall be called the Son of God. And the Lord God shall give unto him the throne of his father David, and he shall reign over the house of Jacob forever, and of his kingdom there shall be no end." (Luke i:35, 32,33.)

The first Adam was put upon probation; the last Adam was predicted to triumph. The first man is of the earth, earthy; the second man is of heaven. The first man is the family head of earth-born men; the second man is the family-head of spirit-born men. As Paul suggests when he says that Adam was a type, a resemblance, of him that was to come. (Rom. v:14.) The idea that Christ is the head of a family, is in accord with Scripture. Isaiah says (liii:10): "When thou shalt make his soul an offering for sin *he shall see his seed*, he shall prolong his days, and the pleasure of the Lord shall prosper in his hand." Every regenerate soul is of the seed of Christ, and is a member of the spiritual family of Christ.

If Paul had omitted the words "as" and "so," and, changing the construction of the verse somewhat, simply written: Through Adam all men were condemned, and through the Christ all the same men shall be justified, he would have given an argument and declaration of mankind's universal justification, which no skill of man could overthrow. But he did not so write.

And his purpose in Rom. v:18 doubtless was, not to make an argument for universal justification, but, by declaration of truth, to magnify the Christ, and declare the justification of all the people of Christ.

Other answers are given by evangelical Christians, but that the difference of numbers is the true answer, is confirmed by the following facts:

1. When Paul says, " Even so through one act of righteousness the free gift came unto all men to justification of life" (v:18 R. V.) he teaches that each one of these all men is, sooner or later, to possess a state of justification before God. In the first half of the verse where he says, "Judgment came unto all men to condemnation," the condemnatory judgment was an actual fact, showing itself in the experience of mankind. It fastened itself upon every child of the first Adam. "As it is written, There is none righteous, no, not one," just so Paul teaches that, as an actual fact, each one of the second " all men " of verse 18, shall experience a state of justifica-

tion. As the all men of the first clause have a certain experience, so the all men of the second clause have a certain experience. It is as real in the one case as in the other. It is the prediction of one under the inspiration of God. God, who sees the end from the beginning, instructs his inspired one to teach that as a certain "all men" came into condemnation, so a certain "all men" came into justification of life. There was no difficulty in God's so instructing his prophet. The entire conduct of every person is plain to the eye of God. "All things are naked and laid open before the eyes of Him with whom we have to do." (Heb. iv:13.)

God here substantially says, "A certain 'all men' shall receive my gospel, and be justified, and constitute my church on earth." No believer in God and revelation should hesitate to receive a saying like this, from God. It is very much on a par with the prediction of Christ where he says, "Upon this rock I will build my church; and the gates of Hades shall not prevail against it." This last prediction calls for God's oversight as really as the other. Both predictions say, The race of Christian believers shall not fail. Both predictions shall be made good by the work of the Holy Ghost on human hearts. I see no more difficulty in believing the one than the other. The "all men" justified constitute from age to age the church of Jesus Christ.

2. A careful notice of Paul's series of contrasted opposites leads to the conclusion that the "all men" of the second clause are actually justified.

In verse 16, he mentions the judgment, and its opposite, the free gift. Also, in verse 16, the result of the judgment—condemnation, and the result of the free gift—justification.

In verse 17, the result of the judgment—the reign of death, and the result of the free gift—its recipients reigning in life.

In verse 18, the result of one trespass—all men condemned, and the result of one act of righteousness—all men justified.

In verse 19, the result of one man's disobedience—the many made sinners, and the result of the obedience of one—the many made righteous.

Here are four pairs of contrasted opposites. And in each of these four pairs of opposites the first of the two things mentioned is an actual experience of men. Condemnation—the reign of death—all men condemned—the many made sinners—these four things actually take hold of men, and bring men under their power.

And these four things are uniform in power. When one is effective, all are effective. Now in these four pairs, the principle that applies to the first of the two things mentioned, applies also to the second of the two things mentioned. That is to say, if in the series of four opposites any one of the second of the two things mentioned is an actual fact in the experience of men, then the other three of the things mentioned second in the series are also actual facts in the experience of men. The law that runs through the first things in the four pairs, must run through the second things in the four pairs.

Now the second thing of the pair in verse 17, is an actual fact in the experience of men —those who receive the free gift reign in life, and some receive it, therefore the three other of the second things mentioned are also actual facts in the experience of men. And so when in the series of second things mentioned Paul says, " The free gift came unto all men unto justification of life," the meaning is—the free gift unto justification of life enters into the actual experience of the " all men " mentioned. It takes hold of them and brings them graciously under its power. It secures their justification. As says the prophet, " Thy people shall be willing in the day of thy power." (Ps. cx:3). Again, in these pairs, opposite things are contrasted. Now the opposite of condemnation is more than justification offered, it is justification effected.

3. In v. 18, Paul says—the judgment came unto condemnation—and the free gift came unto justification of life. Now in Chap. vi: 23, Paul states that the free gift of God is eternal life in Christ Jesus our Lord. Therefore, when the free gift effects justification, it brings the soul into a state of eternal life. The free gift of God justifies the soul, and blesses it with eternal life. Who are the souls thus blessed? They are the "all men" mentioned second in Rom. v:18. As the "all men" first mentioned experience the condemnation; so, the "all men" mentioned second, experience the justification and eternal life. It is not simply life for a year, nor for a century, but it is eternal life. It abides with the soul when it passes over into the heavenly glory. "The gifts and calling of God are without repentance." (Rom. xi:29.)

The water which Christ has given each of these souls to drink, has become in them a well of water springing up into everlasting life. And these souls will never know thirst again (John iv:14.)

Now, in case we say the second "all men"

of Rom. v:18 are equal in number to the first "all men" of that verse, what is this but to say that Paul teaches Universalism?

Therefore, the right answer to the Universalist argument from Rom. v:18 is, the number of the second "all men" is less than the number of the first "all men."

4. A parallel statement which helped us in ascertaining the inequality of the two "alls" will also help in ascertaining whether the justification of life is merely offered, or actually bestowed of God, and possessed by its recipients.

"As by the unwise management of Dr. A, all the inmates of the hospital suffered loss; so, by the wise management of Dr. B, all the inmates of the hospital experienced benefit."

Here, in the first place, loss was an actual experience of all the inmates under Dr. A. And in the second place, benefit was an actual experience of all the inmates under Dr. B.

They were not merely offered benefit. They received benefit. Just so in Paul's statement in Rom. v:18, where he says, "The free gift came upon all men to justification of life." The great benefit is not merely offered to the "all men," but is bestowed upon them of God. They receive it and become justified in God's sight.

Paul, as an inspired man, knew the meaning of words and the method of constructing sentences; and we say here without fear of successful contradiction, that the method in which he has constructed his sentence in Rom. v:18, demands that the second "all men" mentioned receive and possess justification of life.

5. A right understanding of the statement in v. 20, "grace did abound more exceedingly," confirms the belief that the second "all men" of Rom. v:18 are justified and everlastingly saved.

"Where sin abounded grace did much more abound." The abounding of sin is the prevailing of sin. Sin did not abound so long as our first parents were merely tempted to sin. But sin abounded when the temptation took effect, and sin was enacted. Sin abounded when our first parents, under temptation, chose to sin, and thereby came under its power. Sin, then, reigned over them. The abounding of sin is the reigning of sin. Now, among mankind the opposite thing to the abounding of sin is the abounding of grace. These two things are opposites. Now grace merely offered is not an opposite to the abounding of sin. Grace may be offered and sin may abound, at the same time, in reference to the same persons. Grace was offered and sin abounded in the multitudes who rejected Noah's preaching, and perished in the deluge. In reference to those multitudes, disobedient and unbelieving, it cannot be truthfully said that grace abounded. And why? Because offered grace is not abounding grace. Just as where sin abounds it reigns, so where grace abounds it reigns. Just as where sin abounds it brings the soul under its power, so where grace abounds it brings the soul under its power. Abounding grace is winning grace, successful grace. Grace abounded with Noah, with Abraham, with David, with Paul. And not with Cain, and not with Esau, and not with Judas. Now, grace abounds in them who are connected with Christ. Adam's trespass makes sin abound. And Christ's righteousness makes grace abound. The one opens the floodgate of sin; the other opens the floodgate of righteousness. Adam's trespass makes sin abound in the case of the "all men" mentioned first in Rom. v:18. And Christ's righteousness makes grace abound in the case of the "all men" mentioned second in Rom. v:18. The first "all men" comprise all the descendants of Adam. The second "all men" comprise all the redeemed of Christ. The first "all men" are connected with Adam by natural descent. The second "all men" are connected with Christ by the grace of God, and the Holy Spirit's power. "Which were born not of blood, nor of the will of the flesh, nor of the will of man, but of God." (John i:13.) There are two multitudes. The head of the first multitude is Adam. The head of the second multitude is Christ. As Paul says, "The head of every man is Christ." (I Cor. xi:3.) And as Christ, the head, has entered heaven, so will every one of whom he is the head ultimately enter there. "The Lord will give grace *and* glory." (Ps. lxxxiv:11.)

6. That grace abounding means—not grace offered, but—grace taking effect, is fully confirmed by Paul's idea of abounding grace as set forth in II Cor. ix:8. He says: "God is able to make all grace abound toward you; that ye, always having all sufficiency in all things, may abound to every good work." Now, when all grace abounded toward the Corinthians, it was Paul's idea that the Corinthians would abound to every good work. The grace abounding results in generosity of heart, in a Christ-like disposition. And Paul makes this indisputable by his quotation from Ps. cxii:9, which immediately follows. He quotes (v. 9): "As it is written, He [the good

man, the man with whom grace abounds] hath dispersed abroad; he hath given to the poor; his righteousness remaineth forever." Here we see that grace abounding, not only takes effect, but takes effect forever.

And so the real meaning of Rom. v:18 is— As through Adam's trespass the judgment came upon all his children (the earth-born) to condemnation; even so through Christ's righteousness the free gift came upon all his children (the spirit-born) to justification of life. " Behold, I, and the children which God hath given me." (Heb. ii:13).

7. In Rom. iv:25 Paul, speaking of Christ says, " Who was delivered up for our trespasses, and was raised for our justification." (Rev. Ver.) By common consent the justification of this verse is the justification of believers, and is connected with pardon and a title to everlasting life. Now, the justification of Rom. v:18 is the same justification. It is signified by the same Greek word (dikaiōsis) and should be considered as having the same meaning, unless some good reason can be given to the contrary. In both cases the justification comes through Christ. Now, no person having justification through Christ remains in unbelief. For we are "justified by faith," and "he that believeth not is con-

demned already." (John iii:18.) There is no middle state between justification by faith, and condemnation because of unbelief. Men, hearing the gospel and knowing the difference between right and wrong, are either believers or unbelievers; and thus are either in a state of justification or condemnation. The man in unbelief—the condemned man—cannot be in a state of justification. But the second "all men" of Rom. v:18, are in a state of justification. Therefore, being in a state of justification, they are believers—they are the saved ones of Christ.

8. The justification of Rom. v:18 is a justification of life, and comes through the redeeming work of Christ. Now, wherever life is spoken of as coming through the redeeming work of Christ, it means salvation. The resurrection of life (John v:29), is a resurrection unto everlasting salvation; and justification of life, a result of Christ's redeeming work, is justification unto everlasting salvation. Therefore, the second "all men" of Rom. v:18, possessing justification of life, are to be everlastingly saved.

Rom. v:19. For as through the one man's disobedience the many were made sinners; even so through the obedience of the one shall the many be made righteous.

The Universalist argument from this verse is as follows: The "many" in both clauses of the verse includes the entire human race. And then the verse asserts that the entire human race shall be made righteous; and consequently saved.

Two differing answers are given by evangelical Christians to this argument. One answer is: While the first many includes all mankind, yet the number in the second many is less than the number in the first many; and consequently, Paul does not assert that all mankind shall be made righteous.

The second answer is—The persons of each "many" are equal in number, including all mankind; but being "made righteous" is conditional on faith in Christ, and since some do not believe in Christ, they therefore fail to be "made righteous," and saved.

We believe the following reasons fully maintain the correctness of the first answer:

1. The verse permits the opinion that the numbers of the second "many" may be less than the numbers of the first "many." This has been shown in our remarks on Rom. v:18.

2. Paul's regular flow of thought, and method of contrasting opposites will also help us here. In v. 19 the persons who were

made sinners are the ones over whom sin abounded, as mentioned in v. 20. And the ones over whom sin abounded, as mentioned in v. 20, are the ones over whom sin reigned in or unto death, as mentioned in v. 21. Just so the persons mentioned in v. 19 as "made righteous" are the persons over whom grace much more abounds, as mentioned in v. 20. And the persons over whom grace much more abounds, as mentioned in v. 20, are the same persons over whom grace reigns unto eternal life through righteousness. Now the persons over whom grace reigns unto eternal life through righteousness are saved forever. Therefore the persons "made righteous," being the same persons as those over whom grace reigns unto eternal life, are saved forever.

In v. 19 the first multitude (the many) are the condemned; the second multitude (the many) are the justified. In v. 20 the first multitude are under sin, and the second multitude are under grace. In v. 21 sin reigns over the first multitude unto death; and grace reigns over the second multitude unto eternal life. In each of these three verses the fallen multitude is contrasted with the rescued multitude. The fallen multitude is connected with the first Adam, a disobedient soul. And the rescued multitude is connected with the second Adam—the Lord from heaven—a life-giving Spirit. Sin and death go down from the first Adam to his multitude. Life and righteousness go down from the second Adam to his multitude. Believe in the second Adam as a crucified and divine redeemer, and you will be included in his multitude.

3. Paul teaches in Rom. vi:23, that eternal life is the gift of God. And John teaches that God hath given to us eternal life. (I John, v:11.) Now if God gave to John and the Christians to whom he wrote eternal life, then he can just as readily bestow eternal life upon that "many" of whom Paul affirms "they shall be made righteous." And when God bestows eternal life upon that "many" there will be no difficulty concerning their faith in Christ. After a soul has heard of Christ, faith in him is inseparable from the eternal life which God bestows. The demand for faith is met in God's bestowment of eternal life.

The soul on which God has bestowed eternal life is born of the Spirit. As says the apostle, "which were born, not of blood, nor of the will of the flesh, nor of the will of man, but of God." (John i:13.) And the Spirit has taken of the things of Christ and showed them unto that soul. And "the fruit of the Spirit is love, joy, peace, long suffering, gentleness, goodness, *faith.*"

And when the soul exercises *faith* it will be justified and made righteous. It is thus clearly within the power of Almighty God to fulfil the prediction of his inspired servant. And all of us should put our trust in God as a God of truth. "Hath he spoken and shall he not make it good?" (Num. xxiii:19).

4. Paul teaches that God quickened—made alive—the Ephesian Christians, when they were dead in sins, for his great love wherewith he loved them. Now after God wrought that gracious work upon them they were "saints" and "faithful in Christ," and they chose to believe in Jesus. And since Paul says it is to be by the obedience of the Christ that this "many" shall be made righteous; and since Isaiah says, "My righteous servant shall justify many; for he shall bear their iniquities" (liii:11,) we, therefore, conclude that the "many" whom Paul says shall be made righteous, and the "many" whom God's righteous servant shall justify, are the same persons; and that as the purchase of the blood unto death of his righteous Son, God loves them with his great love.

Therefore on account of his great love wherewith he loves them he will quicken them— make them alive—even though he finds them dead in trespasses and sins. And being made alive, unbelief shall be banished, they shall hear the good Shepherd's voice, and become obedient to his call. They shall believe—be justified—made righteous—and saved.

5. God promised Christ a great reward for his obedience unto death. He said, "I will divide him a portion with the great, and he shall divide the spoil with the strong, because he hath poured out his soul unto death." (Isa. liii:12.)

God here virtually says, — Because of Christ's obedience unto death I will give to him many rescued and saved souls.

Paul virtually says, By the obedience of Christ unto death many souls shall be justified and made righteous. And it is reasonable to conclude that the many souls which God promised to Christ, are the same "many" whom Paul says shall be justified and made righteous by the obedience of the Christ. And the eternal "God who quickeneth the dead and calleth those things that be not as though they were," and with whom all things are possible, can and surely will make his promise good.

And Christ himself says, All that the Father giveth me shall come to me ; and him that cometh to me I will in no wise cast out. (Jno. vi:37). Now it is reasonable to conclude that those given by the Father to Christ, and who, as Christ says, shall come unto him, are the very ones whom Paul says "shall be made righteous." And they who come to Christ and whom he will not cast out, shall be everlastingly saved. Therefore it is reasonable to conclude that the many who "shall be made righteous" will be everlastingly saved.

6. From Paul's statement in Rom. viii:30, we infer that those who are once "made righteous" reach the heavenly glory. For those "made righteous" are justified, and, " whom he justified them he also glorified."

7. It is reasonable to conclude that the "many" whom Paul says "shall be made righteous," are the " many sons" whom God is bringing to glory after making the Captain of their salvation " perfect through sufferings." (Heb. ii:10.) And when these "many sons" get to glory, as they doubtless will, then the " many" who shall be " made righteous " will also possess the heavenly glory.

8. Paul says, " By grace ye are saved" (Eph. ii:5). If saved by grace, then most cer-

tainly saved by exceedingly abounding grace. Now in reference to whom does Paul say, Grace abounds more exceedingly? Plainly in reference to the "many" whom the previous verse says "shall be made righteous." By one man's disobedience the many were made sinners,—then sin abounded. By one man's obedience many shall be made righteous,—here grace abounds—grace reigns unto eternal life through righteousness. In and over whom? Plainly in and over the "many" who "shall be made righteous." Therefore the "many" who "shall be made righteous," will be everlastingly saved.

Paul further says, "The grace of our Lord abounded exceedingly" (I Tim. i:14, R. V.) Now very happily we know the spiritual condition of the person to whom the Lord's grace abounded exceedingly. Before the grace abounded he was a persecutor, and injurious. After the grace abounded he was enlightened and believing, and pardoned and saved. Here we have a particular instance where grace abounding exceedingly wrought salvation. Now, since in Paul's case, grace abounding exceedingly wrought salvation, we are fully entitled to conclude that in all cases where grace abounds exceedingly it will effect salvation. And since grace abounded exceedingly in the case of the second "many" of Rom. v:18, that is, the "many" that "shall be made righteous," we therefore conclude that that many will be everlastingly saved. We now invite those who affirm that in all cases grace may exceedingly abound and yet fail to effect salvation, to produce from the Scriptures a single instance where grace exceedingly abounds toward a person and that person remains unbelieving, impenitent, and unsaved. Now if "the many" who "shall be made righteous" and who are to be saved, include all mankind without exception, how then can we escape the conclusion that Paul in Rom. v:19 teaches Universalism.

9. Paul asks, "Shall we continue in sin that grace may abound?" (Rom. vi:1). The "we" are Christians and pardoned since they "died to sin." The question then is, Shall we, who are Christians, continue to sin, that grace may abound? Now in this question do the words "grace may abound" signify pardon may be offered, or, grace may be victorious? Christians who are dead to sin would not put the question—Shall we who are Christians continue in sin that pardon may be offered? There would be no sense in such a question, for Christians are

already pardoned. But tempted Christians might easily put the question—Shall we continue in sin that grace may triumph over our sins—may win greater victories? Paul entreats them not to continue in sin, since sin is contrary to their new nature. They have been united to Christ, and just as he was raised from the dead to a new life, so they should walk in newness of life. Do not sin in order that grace may triumph over your sins, for sinning is contrary to your new spiritual nature. This is sound reasoning. But to say to pardoned men, Do not continue in sin in order that pardon may be offered, is weak, and beneath the intelligence of the apostle. The words then, "Grace may abound" signify grace may be victorious. And so when Paul says, Where sin abounded grace did much more abound, he teaches that those with whom grace abounds will be won by grace, and grace, will reign over them, and they will be saved. And grace certainly abounds with the "made righteous." And those "made righteous" will certainly be saved.

I Cor. xv:22, "For as in the Adam all die, so also in the Christ shall all be made alive." (We follow the original Greek by inserting the definite article before Adam and Christ.)

Here again, just as in Rom. v:18, there is no necessity that the number in the one "all" equal the number in the other "all." The "all" made alive may be less in number than the "all" that die. Who are the all that die? The natural posterity of Adam; and not the angels, and not the inhabitants of any other world. Why his natural posterity "all die"? Because they were in him. They were in him as Levi was in Abraham when the latter paid tithes to Melchizedek. As says the Scriptures, "He was yet in the loins of his father whem Melchizedek met him," (Heb. vii:10.) And Levi, as says the Scriptures, "through Abraham hath paid tithes," and shared with his father Abraham the latter's inferiority to Melchizedek who received the tithes. He was in him, and was in condition like him. The natural posterity, then, are in the progenitor, and share the progenitor's condition. Putting this idea into the first part of the parallel, it says:

In the Adam were his natural posterity, and they all share his condition. And Adam's condition, through his transgression, is one of death. It then says, " In the Adam were his natural posterity, and they all die." But Adam was of earth, and Christ was of heaven. The first man Adam became a living soul.

The last man Adam became a life giving spirit. And therefore, to Adam's natural posterity corresponds Christ's spiritual seed. The spiritual seed share Christ's condition. And since through obedience, he has been made alive, therefore, they also shall be made alive. Putting now the two parts of the parallel together, we have the following: For as in the Adam were his natural posterity, and they all die, so also in the Christ are his spiritual seed, and they all shall be made alive.

But is it scriptural to speak of Christ's spiritual seed, and of their being in him?

Yes, for Paul says, " If any man be in Christ he is a new creature;" and, " I knew a man in Christ." Being in Christ that man was a new creature, a regenerated man, a spiritual son. Abbreviating the sentence somewhat, we have: For as in the Adam all his natural posterity die, so also in the Christ all his spiritual seed shall be made alive. This is the meaning of the verse. But there is here no information as to the equality of the two numbers. And the comparison is, not concerning the number of the two multitudes, but concerning the Adam and the Christ; and concerning the universality of the influence of each of them over their respective multitudes. As Adam is a fountain of power, so Christ is a fountain of power. As Adam is a fountain of death-bringing power, so Christ is a fountain of life-giving power. As Adam is a fountain of death to *all* in him, so Christ is a fountain of life to *all* in him. But there is nothing here that moulds into equality of number the "all in Adam," and the "all in Christ." The verse, therefore, furnishes no proof of universal salvation.

Perhaps by the following parallel the idea may be brought out still more clearly:

As in the polar regions all are influenced by the cold, so in the equatorial regions all are influenced by the heat.

Who are influenced by the cold?

Those who are in the polar regions, and *all* those who are in the polar regions. Who are influenced by the heat? Those who are in the equatorial regions, and *all* those who are in the equatorial regions.

Are the two peoples in these two regions the very same in person and in number? Concerning that, the sentence *has nothing to say*. In like manner, in the sentence, As in Adam all die, so in Christ shall all be made alive; concerning equality of the two numbers, the sentence *has nothing to say*. But the context and other Scriptures have something to say.

The subject on which Paul was throwing the light of his inspiration was: What the future has in store for them that "are fallen asleep in Christ"? Though asleep—though deceased—they were believers; they were and are in Christ; being in him, and he has been made alive, they shall share his condition—they shall experience his life-giving power—they all shall be made alive. Yea, *all* who are in him shall be made alive. Through their faith they were proved to be in Christ; and being in him, they are within the reach of his life-giving power. But elsewhere the Scriptures tell us that "all men have not faith." And Christ tells us: Whosoever shall deny me before men, him will I also deny before my Father which is heaven.

But if Paul in the last "all" of the comparison had no reference to "all of human kind," why did he not say "some" instead of "all?" Had he there said "some" instead of "all," he would have failed to affirm the truth that all who are in Christ shall be made alive. He would have permitted the thought that some who are in Christ may remain forever under the power of death.

As follows: As in the Adam all his natural posterity die, so also in the Christ shall some of his spiritual seed be made alive. What then, becomes of the rest of Christ's spiritual seed? For all that Paul would then in the passage say to the contrary, they might remain forever under the power of death. That is just what he was opposing with all the power of his inspiration. And he must say "all" in order to affirm that Christ's life-giving power reaches every one of his seed. Alive or dead, all believers are the Lord's; and shall be made alive—the living, at Christ's coming, by the blessed transformation—the dead, at Christ's coming, by the blessed resurrection. "It is enough for the disciple that he be *as* his master, and the servant *as* his lord."

Taking a hint from Paul, it may be proper to compare the Adam and the Christ to two olive trees. The Adam a wild olive tree; the Christ a good olive tree. Each of these trees bears fruit after its kind. The wild olive bears wild fruit; the good olive bears good fruit. And then we have the following comparison:

As in the wild olive tree, all fruit is wild in kind; so in the good olive tree, all fruit is good in kind. In this comparison the "all fruit" first mentioned is all the fruit growing on the wild olive tree; and *only* all the fruit growing on that tree. And the "all fruit" next mentioned is all the fruit growing on the good olive tree; and *only* all the fruit growing on that good tree. And in like manner in the comparison of I Cor. xv:22, the "all" first mentioned is all mankind springing by nature from Adam, and only that all. And the "all" next mentioned is all mankind springing by grace from Christ, and *only* that all. The one "all" is natural born mankind. The other "all" is spiritual born mankind. And therefore we are not justified in concluding that these two multitudes are equal in number until we can prove from some other Scripture that all mankind, without exception, are or will be spirit born.

We mention but one more parallel statement, as follows:

As in air all men receive good; so in liquor all men shall receive harm. In construction, this sentence is a parallel to I Cor. xv:22. And if this sentence does not assert that all men shall receive harm through liquor, then I Cor. xv:22 does not assert that all men shall be made alive through Christ. What this sentence does assert is—not that all men shall be in liquor (intoxicated) and thus receive harm—but that all men in liquor (intoxicated) shall receive harm. These two things are very different. The one is an affirmation that all men shall be intoxicated and receive harm. The other is an affirmation that all men who become intoxicated shall receive harm. A difference numerically of millions. Before receiving the harm a condition is implied, that of being in liquor. If they be in liquor, all men shall receive harm. And it is not implied that all men are in this condition. Now since this condition is implied in the case of harm, let us insert it in the sentence, as follows: As in air all men receive good, so if they be in liquor, all men shall receive harm. This means, in other words, as in air all men receive good, so all men who are in liquor shall receive harm.

This, the true meaning of the clause, does not assert that all men shall be in liquor, and thus receive harm. But "all who are in liquor," without saying how many they are, shall receive harm.

A condition is also implied in the first clause of the sentence. When it says—As in air all men receive good, it is implied that the men who receive the good, are in the air —breathing it.

But it is not asserted that all men are in air—breathing it, and receiving the good. Some men may be deprived of it by steam, or gas, or drowning, or hanging.

The clause then really asserts that all men who are in air, receive good.

Putting together, then, what the two clauses really mean, we have the following:

As all men who are in air, receive good, so all men who are in liquor, shall receive harm.

This is the true meaning of the sentence—As in air all men receive good, so in liquor all men shall receive harm.

And just so by parity of reasoning, the true meaning of the sentence, "As in Adam all die, so in Christ all shall be made alive," is—As all who are in Adam die, so, all who are in Christ, shall be made alive.

2. Another proof that I Cor. xv:22 affirms the living again of only the dead in Christ, is found in the word employed to indicate the character of that resurrection. When the good who sleep in the grave, experience the resurrection, it is the resurrection of zōe—life. When they that have done evil, experience their resurrection, it is the resurrection of krisis—condemnation. As Christ teaches in John v:28,29, where he says: "The hour is coming in the which all that are in the graves, shall hear his voice, and shall come forth; they that have done good, unto the resurrection of life (zōe), and they that have done evil, unto the resurrection of damnation

(krisis). Now, the word translated "made alive"— zōopoieo — has zōe to indicate its character; not krisis; and thus indicates that it is the blessed resurrection.

3. Again, Christ says (John x:10) : "I am come that they might have life—zōe." Now, this life is the blessing which Christ bestows upon the believing and obedient. It is therefore manifestly improper to ascribe this life (zōe) to the wicked in their resurrection. And thus the resurrection of 1 Cor. xv:22, having zōe, Christ's blessing, in it, does not include the impenitent dead.

4. In John iii:36 the Lord teaches that they who do not believe in him, shall not see zōe—life. Now, to affirm that those who shall be made alive—shall be granted life—spoken of in I Cor. xv:22, include the dead rejecters of Christ, is to affirm (however ignorantly) directly the opposite of the teaching of the Lord. It is to say that they who die in unbelief and sin, shall see zōe—life. For zōe—life—marks the character of the resurrection of I Cor. xv:22.

5. The usage, in other parts of the New Testament, of the word translated "made alive," confirms the belief that it is used in I Cor. xv:22 only of those who are united to Christ. The word is zōopoieo, and means to

make alive, to grant life to, to quicken. It occurs in Gal. iii:21 : "Is the law then against the promises of God? God forbid; for if there had been a law given which could have given life (zōopoieo), verily righteousness should have been by the law." Here the word indicates a life promised of God—holy, happy, eternal—belonging only to the people of God. It occurs in Rom. iv:17 : " He (Abraham) believed God, who quickeneth (zōopoieo) the dead." In obedience to God's command Abraham was about to slay Isaac, his son, believing that God would raise him from the dead. What kind of a resurrection did Abraham trust in God that Isaac would have? Plainly a happy one, since he was an obedient child of a believing father—a true member of the Church of God. Here the word zōopoieo, to quicken, make alive, doubtless indicates a happy resurrection.

It occurs in II Cor. iii:6 : "Who also made us sufficient as ministers of a new covenant; not of the letter, but of the spirit; for the letter killeth, but the spirit giveth life (zōopoieo). (Rev. Ver.)

Here it indicates the life, that is, the salvation which the spirit of the new covenant gives.

It occurs in I Pet. iii:18 : "Christ * * * being put to death in the flesh, but quickened (zōopoieo) by the Spirit." Here the word indicates the glorious resurrection of the Christ. Now, surely Paul would not take a word that indicates the glorious resurrection of the Christ, that indicates the salvation which the spirit of the new covenant gives, that indicates the happy resurrection of a son wonderful in obedience and faith, that indicates a life that no law given could procure, and apply that word of glory to the resurrection of the unrighteous dead—the resurrection of the enemies of God.

It occurs in Rom. viii:11 : "But if the spirit of him that raised up Jesus from the dead, dwell in you, he that raised up Christ from the dead, shall also quicken (zōopoieo) your mortal bodies by his Spirit that dwelleth in you."

Here the word indicates the happy resurrection of the bodies of believers. And that happy resurrection is conditioned on the previous indwelling of the Spirit of God. Hence it is manifestly improper, without producing a "Thus saith the Lord," to assert that this same word indicates the resurrection of the bodies of the unrighteous dead. To do so, is to obliterate the distinction between the destinies of the righteous and the wicked. Hence Paul includes in the "shall

all be made alive" (zōopoieo) of I Cor. xv:22, only them that have believed in Jesus.

It occurs in I Cor. xv:45 : "The first man Adam, became a living soul. The last Adam became a life-giving (zōopoieo) spirit." (Rev. Ver.) Here it indicates the life which Christ as a Saviour, bestows upon his people.

And indicating thus the full salvation of the Christian, it does not seem possible that it indicates a life to be bestowed upon the wicked dead. But if it does, then how can we escape the conclusion that Paul teaches Universalism?

6. Another argument that zōopoieo indicates the bodily resurrection of only the righteous, is based on its meaning when united to the Greek preposition syn—with forming the word syzōopoieo, which means, to make alive with. It occurs in Eph. ii:5 ; "God who is rich in mercy, for his great love wherewith he loved us, even when we were dead in sins, hath *quickened* us together with Christ." Here it signifies regeneration—the new birth—the resulting act of God's great love—the greatest act of blessing which God works for a human soul during its earthly journey. And probably the greatest blessing bestowed upon it for all eternity ; since it starts the soul upon a course of everlasting

goodness and joy. As says John the Apostle (Epis. I iii:9): "Whosoever is born of God doth not commit sin; for his seed remaineth in him; and he cannot sin, because he is born of God." God be thanked for that *whosoever*. It occurs in Col. ii:13: "And you, being dead in your sins and the uncircumcision of your flesh, hath he (God) *quickened*—made alive—together with him (Christ), having forgiven you all trespasses." Here also it signifies the new birth—a spiritual making-alive—bringing the soul into harmony and union with a holy and resurrected Christ. Now, the meaning of zōopoieo by being joined to syn—with, is not changed any further than this that the blessing is experienced together with—in company with—some one else. Here, in these two instances, with Christ. Now, can we think that Paul, unless he was a Universalist, would take a word that indicates the greatest blessing that God works out for a human soul, and use that word to indicate an act wrought upon the bodies of the impenitent and wicked dead? And now, to offset all these powerful arguments not one specific instance can be mentioned where zōopoieo is used to indicate the bodily resurrection of a person who died in unbelief and sin. We, therefore, conclude that the second "all" of I Cor. xv:22, includes only those who are united to Christ by the work of the Holy Ghost.

7. The resurrection of the latter part of the chapter is admitted by all believers to be a resurrection of blessed life. Now, the resurrection foretold in the 22d verse, is the same as is described in the latter part of the chapter. This is made plain by the fact that the happy resurrection in the latter part of the chapter is the harvest of which Christ is the first fruits. And the harvest and the first fruits are of the same nature. Since Paul says in Rom. xi:16: "If the first fruit be holy, the lump is also holy." Now, Christ is mentioned as the first fruits of them that slept, in the 20th verse; and after Christ has so been mentioned, all affirmations concerning the resurrection must be considered as belonging to Christ's people, unless special mention is made of the wicked. Paul makes no such special mention. Therefore the affirmation in verse 22 of—shall be made alive—shall be granted life—must be considered as belonging to Christ's people; and as affirming a happy resurrection. It is the happy resurrection harvest, following the resurrection of Christ—the first fruits. The fuller description in the latter part of the chapter is only

OF DIVINE GRACE.   175

the unfolding of the characteristics of the glorious life foretold in the 22d verse.

8. We have seen by the testimony of the Scriptures that the second "all" of I Cor. xv:22, that is, the all who are in Christ, are to be everlastingly saved. Now if that second all includes all mankind, then we see no escape from the conclusion that Paul teaches that all mankind will be forever saved—that is, that Universalism is true.

But all evangelicals (rightly according to the Scriptures) deny that Universalism is true. We therefore conclude that the second "all"—the all who are in Christ—does not include all mankind without exception. Who then are the "all" who are in Christ? They are the reward which God gives the Christ for his willing yet painful obedience unto death.

Christ says, " Lo, I come (in the volume of the book it is written of me) to do thy will, O God." (Heb. x:7.) God says, "I will divide him a portion with the great, and he shall divide the spoil with the strong, because he hath poured out his soul unto death." (Isa. liii:12)

Is there a man in all the church of God who would wish that reward uncertain? Is there a man in all the church of God who wishes the Almighty to refrain from putting forth his mighty power, and thus to allow Christ, through human perversity, to fail of his well-earned reward? God forbid. We have seen that God promised Christ a reward. Now will not God make his promise good? Shall Christ perform the work and earn the wages, and God refuse the payment?

Christ has performed the condition; shall God refuse to grant what the performance of the condition calls for? Nay, verily, for this would be to break Christ's heart a second time. A second time to make him cry, My God, my God, why hast thou forsaken me? Christ's reward is the everlasting salvation of the transgressors for whom he intercedes. (Isa. liii:12; John xi:42.) To refuse him this, is to act worse than any honest employer of the lowliest day laborer. Moral obligation—common honesty, demands that he should have his reward. But, does some one say, The reward is beyond God's power to bestow; since God cannot enter the human will, and cannot to a certainty lead human souls to believe in, and love and serve the Lord Jesus. He can entreat; He cannot control. Remember, objector, that God has promised to control.

"He shall see of the travail of his soul, and shall be satisfied; by his knowledge shall my righteous servant justify many; for he shall bear their iniquities. Therefore will I divide him a portion with the great, and he shall divide the spoil with the strong." (Isa. liii: 11, 12.)

Here God promises that Christ's sufferings shall have a satisfactory result—that Christ shall secure the justification of many souls. To satisfy Christ—an eternal king—this must be a justification of life, an eternal salvation. These many justified and saved souls are the portion and reward which God has promised Christ. Now where is the truthfulness of the God of truth if God cannot make his promise good? God's knowledge takes in all events, and when he promised he knew whether or not he could fulfil that promise. He is a God of truth, and he will make it good. The all who are in Christ, then, and who shall be made alive, are the all whom God has given to Christ to be saved. Paul speaks of them as "chosen unto salvation through sanctification of the Spirit and belief of the truth." (II Thess. ii:13.)

Paul speaks of them as God's elect, saying, "Who shall lay anything to the charge of God's elect? It is God that justifieth. Who is he that condemneth? It is Christ that died." (Rom. viii:33, 34.) Christ speaks of them as his sheep, saying, "My sheep hear my voice, and I know them, and they follow me. And I give unto them eternal life; and they shall never perish, neither shall any man pluck them out of my hand. My Father which gave them me is greater than all; and no man is able to pluck them out of my Father's hand." (John x:27-29.) Now, before God gave them to Christ, he purposed to give them. And when he purposed to give them he elected them. The all who are in Christ, then, are the elect of God. These are the elect who, as Christ teaches, cannot be deceived. (Mark xiii:22.) They are "called and chosen and faithful." (Rev. xvii:14.) The doctrine of a divine election, then, is true. And Paul seems to have flying at the peak of his theological tent a flag, bearing emblems of a divine election, and a divine and saving power. He seems to regard divine election as a prelude to divine mercy. With him divine election is a fountain of mercy and everlasting salvation. How wide-reaching the streams of this fountain, probably no one knows but God and Jesus. But they reach, and will reach so widely among needy humanity, that Jesus is satisfied. And in this matter, with what satisfies Christ his people should be satisfied. In this matter

Paul sat at the feet of God and Jesus as a little child. He is an example for us. And every believer shall be ultimately satisfied. "There is a river the streams whereof shall make glad the city of God." (Ps. xlvi:4.)

Is not that river the happy purpose of our God to have mercy and to save? And doubtless, as a result of this good purpose divine joy flowed through all the being of God. His "delights were with the sons of men." (Prov. viii:31.) That purpose gave us Jesus; that purpose gave us pardon; that purpose gave us a regenerated nature; that purpose will give us heaven; that purpose will give every believer in Christ an everlasting salvation. That purpose made Jesus the Head of a multitudinous race redeemed forever. God has made with his beloved Son "an everlasting covenant, ordered in all things, and sure." (II Sam. xxiii:5.) How then, can any one say, notwithstanding the perfect righteousness and reconciling death of Jesus; notwithstanding his resurrection and intercession, all human souls may everlastingly reject him. In times of old, when God's people were in Egyptian bondage, and the lamb of the passover was killed, the blood of the lamb was surely sprinkled, and where the blood was sprinkled, there was sure deliverance—the angel of death, under orders, to a certainty, not calling at that house. (Ex. xii:21-23, 28.) Just so when Christ "the Lamb slain from the foundation of the world," is put to death, his blood is surely sprinkled. And where his blood is sprinkled, there is—not merely offered, but—sure deliverance. The angel of death, under orders, to a certainty, does not smite the blood-sprinkled soul. Christ, our passover, has been sacrificed for us (I Cor. v:7), and his blood has been sprinkled on human souls. And when Christ, our zōe— our life — shall appear, then shall those blood-sprinkled souls appear with him in glory. (Col. iii:4.) The interpretation is accurate, and the salvation is sure. And Christ says: "Come, ye blessed of my Father, inherit the kingdom prepared for you from the foundation of the world." And when those happy words are spoken, those given by the Father to Christ, have come to Christ. And he has not cast them out, and their salvation is sure. And of all those given by the Father, not one has been left behind. Not one good word has failed of all that the Father promised. Just as all the Israelites left Egyptian bondage, even so all blood-sprinkled souls leave the bondage of sin and Satan. The many for whom Christ specially shed his blood (Matt. xxvi:28), have all been "made righteous." And "the redeemed of the Lord have come to Zion with songs and everlasting joy upon their heads."

1 Cor. xv:26: "The last enemy that shall be abolished, is death."

1. The death spoken of, is physical. The context, preceding and following, shows this very clearly. The question, How are the dead raised up? and With what manner of body do they come? surely referred to the physically dead.

"But now Christ hath been raised from the dead, the first fruits of them that are asleep. For since by man came death, by man came also the resurrection of the dead." Surely, the death from which Christ arose, was not spiritual, but physical death. And consequently it is physical death of which the apostle speaks. This physical death shall be abolished when the resurrection of the physically dead takes place.

2. It is the resurrection of them that sleep in Christ, that is spoken of. And while, of course, a happy resurrection, it does not include the enemies of Christ. The Christian dead—they that died in the Lord—may experience a happy bodily resurrection, even while the wicked dead—those who died in

impenitence—remain under the power of sin and condemnation.

3. Bodily death is the last enemy of the Christian dead, but not the last enemy of them that die in unbelief and sin. Since Christ says: "They that have done good, shall come forth unto the resurrection of life; and they that have done ill, unto the resurrection of judgment." (John v:29. Rev.Ver.)

After the bodily death is abolished, there is no harm for the Christian; but after the bodily death is abolished there is condemnatory judgment—penalty—for the wicked. Therefore Paul is addressing Christians only, since he is addressing those whose last enemy is bodily death. And before I Cor. xv:26 can be fairly claimed as teaching universal salvation, it must be shown that all mankind become, in this life, Christians.

Eph. 1:9,10: "Having made known unto us the mystery of his will, according to his good pleasure which he has purposed in himself; that in the dispensation of the fulness of times he might gather together in one all things in Christ, both which are in heaven, and which are on earth, even in him."

The apostle does not here assert that all things, whether in heaven, or in earth, shall be gathered together into Christ. Such an understanding of his language is opposed by its grammatical construction.

1. In the original, "all" is preceded by the definite article, which makes it certain that a definite "all" is meant.

2. Had Paul meant to assert the gathering together of "all things" into Christ, the word Christ in the original would be in the accusative case, according to the general rule that an adjunct expressing direct limit, or termination, is put in the accusative; whereas now the word is in the dative case, according to the general rule that the place at which is put in the dative.

Paul says, "Gather together in one, *ta panta en to Christo*, the all in Christ;" *not ta panta eis ton Christon*, the all into Christ, and between these different statements the distinction is clear and broad. Notice that the distinction here referred to is clearly made in the following passages of Scripture.

Mark v:13: "And the herd ran violently down a steep place into the sea (the accusative), and were choked in the sea" (the dative). Luke x:5,7: "And into whatsoever house (the accusative) ye enter, first say, Peace be to this house." "And in the same house (the dative) remain."

Luke xii:28: "The grass which to-day is

in the field (the dative), and to-morrow is cast into the oven" (the accusative).

Luke xv: 15,25: "And he sent him into his fields (the accusative) to feed swine. Now his older son was in the field" (the dative).

Acts xvi:6,9: "Forbidden of the Holy Ghost to preach the word in Asia." (The dative.) "Come over into Macedonia (the accusative), and help us."

Acts xvi:32, 34: "They spake unto him the word of the Lord, and to all that were in his house" (the dative). "And when he had brought them into his house" (the accusative).

Acts xvii:10, 17: "Paul and Silas went into the synagogue (the accusative) of the Jews." "Therefore disputed he in the synagogue (the dative) with the Jews."

Acts xviii:19, 26: "He entered into the synagogue (the accusative), and reasoned with the Jews." "He began to speak boldly in the synagogue" (the dative).

From these passages it is plainly to be seen that the name of an object in which something is considered as *being*, is in the original Greek put in the dative case; and also that the name of an object into which something is considered as *entering*, is put in the accusative case. This is the rule, and the few exceptions which may occur, have no power to overthrow the rule. And since there is nothing in the context to forbid the application of the rule in this instance, the rule in this instance must be applied. And therefore the apostle is speaking not of those who are to be brought into Christ, but of those who *are* in Christ. His meaning is "that he might gather together in one all things which are in Christ." The passage, therefore, furnishes no proof of universal salvation, unless it can be proved from other Scripture that all men without exception are, in the apostle's meaning, in Christ. But this cannot be done, since the same apostle says: "If any man be in Christ, he is a new creature;" and of necessity, if he is not a new creature, he is not, in the sense spoken of, in Christ.

Col. i:19, 20: "For it pleased the Father that in him should all fulness dwell. And having made peace through the blood of his cross by him, to reconcile all things unto himself; by him, I say, whether they be things in earth, or things in heaven."

Who are included in the "all things" here spoken of?

1. Those who are included in this "all things," are to be reconciled to God. And, therefore, those moral beings who have never sinned, cannot be included; since reconcilia-

tion necessarily implies previous estrangement. But since in the "all things" of the 16th and 17th verses sinless moral beings are included, therefore the "all things" of our passage has a different meaning from the "all things" of those verses.

2. Since this reconciliation is a result of the peace made "through the blood of his cross," and is effected by Christ, therefore the "all" reconciled must be the Church of Christ—the body of which Christ is the head.

3. Since the "all" here spoken of, is the church of Christ, and the "all" spoken of in Eph. i:10 is also the Church of Christ, therefore the "all" here in Colossians must be coextensive with the "all" in Eph. i:10. But since in Eph. i:10 the "all" means the "all who are in Christ," therefore the "all" here does also mean the "all who are in Christ." And since it is impossible to prove that those who live and die rejecting Christ, are, in the sense of the apostle, in Christ, the passage affords no proof of universal salvation.

I Tim. ii:4: "God our Saviour, who will have all men to be saved, and to come to the knowledge of the truth."

The question here arises as to the meaning of the word translated "will." In the original it is *thelo*. The claim has been made that this word is never applied to God in the Bible except to represent his Will of Purpose and Determination. Could this claim be made good, it would be a powerful argument for universal salvation. But the meaning of the word as used in the following passages of Scripture, shows that this claim has no good basis to rest on.

1. Matt. ix:13. Here the common version reads: "I will have (thelo) mercy and not sacrifice." But the Revised Version translates "I *desire* (*thelo*) mercy, and not sacrifice."

2. The same thing is true of the passage Matt. xii:7.

And in reference to accuracy of translation the Revised Version is superior to the common version.

Also, in these two passages (Matt. ix:13 and xii:7) L. A. Sawyer's translation of the New Testament renders *thelo* by "wish," as follows:

"Go and learn what this means, I 'wish' (thelo) for mercy, and not a sacrifice."

The sentence: "I will have (*thelo*) mercy, and not sacrifice," as used in Matt. ix:13 and xii:7, is a quotation from Hos. vi:6, where it reads, in the common version: "I desired mercy, and not sacrifice." And in the Revised Version: "I desire mercy, and not sacrifice." That is to say, the Greek word *thelo* in Matt. ix:13 and xii:7, is a translation of a Hebrew word (Hos. vi:6), which means desire. So not only the common and revised versions, but the Hebrew Lexicon of Gesenius define the Hebrew word. The same Hebrew word occurs in Job xxxiii:32, where Gesenius and the common and revised versions all translate, "I desire to justify thee." And thus it appears that the inspired Matthew uses *thelo* as the equivalent of a Hebrew word which means to desire. Therefore we conclude that, whether used in reference to man or God, one of the meanings of *thelo* is, to desire.

Further in reference to *thelo* as occurring in Matt. ix:13 and xii:7, we think it far better to translate it by "desire" or "wish" rather than "purpose," because the facts in the case —the statements of the chapter from which the quotation is made clearly show that God's wish or purpose, whichever it was, was not accomplished. God complains that his wish was not carried out. He says, "I desire mercy (or kindness) and not sacrifice; and the knowledge of God more than burnt offerings. But they, like Adam, have transgressed the covenant: there have they dealt treacherously against me. Gilead is a city of them that work iniquity, it is stained with blood." Hosea vi:6-8, R. V.

There were great crimes among priests and people.

This was certainly contrary to God's wish.

He wished them, as he wishes all men, to come to the knowledge of the truth and be saved.

But concerning God's actual "purpose and determination."

> "He sits on no precarious throne,
> Nor borrows leave to be."

I Tim. iv:10. "God is the Saviour of all men, especially of those that believe."

This passage teaches that there are different senses in which God is the Saviour of men. In one sense he is the Saviour of believers; in another sense He is the Saviour of all men. But in what sense He is the Saviour either of the one class or of the other the passage does not affirm. And so long as the passage fails to affirm that He is the Saviour of all men in the sense of saving them everlastingly from perdition in the future life; just so long it will fail as a proof text of universal salvation.

God may properly be called the Saviour of all men because of the bestowment of earthly blessings. "He maketh his sun to rise on the evil and the good, and sendeth rain on the just and the unjust." He feeds, he clothes, he sustains all men. It was to a heathen audience that Paul said, " In him we live and move and have our being." And certainly if all men live, move, and have their being in God or by means of God, it may very properly be said because of these temporal blessings, that he is the Saviour of all men. Because Christ gives and sustains the spiritual and eternal life He is properly called the spiritual and eternal Saviour, so because God gives and sustains the temporal life he is properly called the temporal Saviour. When Moses exclaimed, "Happy art thou, O Israel: who is like unto thee, O people saved by the Lord," Universalists admit that he referred, not to an eternal, but to a temporal salvation. Then God was their Saviour because he gave them temporal blessings, and in like manner he is the Saviour of all men because he gives all men temporal blessings. But his being the Saviour of all men in this sense is certainly no proof that all men in the next life will attain unto holiness and happiness.

2. God may also be appropriately termed the Saviour of all men because he offers to save, and is ready to save, spiritually and eternally, all men who in the appointed method seek his aid.

Between two villages lying on the opposite

banks of a river a ferry is established. This ferry offers and is ready to carry across the river all inhabitants of these villages who pay the passage money. All who pay receive transport, whatever their color, character, or possessions. The fare is low and for the extremely poor there is even provided a fund from which they may draw the amount of their fare. Consequently no single inhabitant who applies is refused. Now should a stranger ask of an inhabitant the following question, "Is this ferry the ferry of the inhabitants of the two villages?" what would he mean by that question? Would he mean necessarily to ask whether all the inhabitants without exception had actually crossed or would actually cross the river by the ferry? Not at all; and probably no man would so understand the question. The question might mean whether the ferry is the property of all the inhabitants. It might mean whether it was the only ferry of the two villages: it might mean whether all, without exception, who desire, are allowed to cross by the ferry. And should the inhabitant reply, "Yes, it is the ferry of all the inhabitants; for all who apply, irrespective of color, character or possessions, are ferried across the river," surely no reasonable man would consider him as making an improper reply. And in like manner because God saves all men who sincerely seek salvation, He is appropriately called the Saviour of all men.

But should the inhabitant reply, "Yes, it is the ferry of all the inhabitants; especially of all who apply for crossing" by what perversity of reasoning could it be affirmed that he asserts the actual crossing of all the inhabitants without exception. Nor does this reply assert the actual application of all the inhabitants for crossing. It simply asserts that in one sense it is the ferry of all the inhabitants, in another sense the ferry of those who apply for ferriage. Those who apply are ferried over, those who do not apply are not. In like manner the same thing may be true of Paul's parallel, "God is the Saviour of all men, especially of those that believe." In one sense the Saviour of all; in another sense the Saviour of believers. But believers are saved eternally, unbelievers are not. The following passages show that the special salvation of believers is not restricted to this present life, but is everlasting. " He that believeth on the Son hath everlasting life." (Jno. iii:36). " Labor not for the meat that perisheth, but for that meat which endureth unto everlasting life." (Jno. vi:27). " Whoso eateth my flesh, and drinketh my blood, hath eternal life; and I will raise him up at the last day." (Jno. vi:54).

Heb. ii:14, 15. "For as much then as the children are partakers of flesh and blood He also himself likewise took part of the same, that through death He might destroy him that hath the power of death, that is, the devil; and deliver them who through fear of death were all their lifetime subject to bondage."

That Christ delivers them who through fear of death were all their lifetime subject to bondage is a blessed fact, yet not therefore a proof of universal salvation. When the distinguished missionary, Livingstone, left Britain for Africa to preach Christ to them who were black and ignorant and degraded, his expected hearers did not include all in the world who were black and ignorant and degraded. They did not include such inhabitants of Cuba, nor of North, nor of South America. The Confederate armies killed on the fields of battle, them who were heroic defenders of the Union, yet no one imagines that they killed all who were heroic defenders of the Union; not Grant, not Sheridan, nor their million of brave followers. The fisherman casts his line or sets his nets in the river to catch them which swim therein;

yet not all without exception, for he expects multitudes to remain uncaught.

In like manner it may be true that while Christ does deliver "them who through fear of death were all their lifetime subject to bondage," yet he does not deliver all men without exception who are so subject to bondage.

2. It was on account of "the children" that Christ took part of flesh and blood, and it is doubtless true that "the children" without exception will experience an actual deliverance. Do "the children" include the entire race of Adam? The children are those mentioned in the 13th verse, which is itself a quotation from Isa. viii:18, where they are not the entire race of Israel, but simply the children of Isaiah, united with him according to God's direction, for prophetical purposes. And the quotation is probably used by the apostle to indicate that as the children which God had given to Isaiah were united with him for prophesy, so the children which God gave to Christ were united with Him for salvation. The children of Isaiah were actual proofs of his prophetic power. So the spiritual children of Christ are actual proofs of His saving power. Now the Scriptures nowhere teach that God has

given all men universally to Christ as "children." They teach the contrary. For "the stone which the builders disallowed, the same is made the head of the corner, and a stone of stumbling, and a rock of offence, even to them which stumble at the word, being disobedient; whereunto also they were appointed." (I Peter ii:7, 8). The children are characterized by similarity of disposition,— by obedience to God. " If any man have not the spirit of Christ he is none of his." (Rom. viii:9). "They that are Christ's have crucified the flesh, with the affections and lusts." (Gal. v-24). " Whosoever shall do the will of God, the same is my brother, and my sister and mother." (Mark iii:35). Besides, the verse immediately following our passage (Heb. ii:16) makes it clear that "the children" are the "seed of Abraham." That verse more correctly translated reads, "For verily he assists not the angels, but he assists the seed of Abraham." "To Abraham and his seed were the promises made." (Gal. iii:16.) And those whom he delivers, are certainly no greater in number than those whom he assists. Now, though the apostle does teach that Christ assists the seed of Abraham, he does *not* teach that Christ assists those who are not the seed of Abraham. And therefore he does not teach that Christ delivers any who are not the seed of Abraham. Now, by no possibility can the seed of Abraham include the whole human race, unless the phrase signifies his spiritual seed. But as signifying the spiritual seed it can include none but those who are Christ's. "And if ye be Christ's, then ye are Abraham's seed." And those who are Christ's, the apostle teaches, have his spirit, and "have crucified the flesh with the affections and lusts." They are believers. "That he (Abraham) might be the father of all them that believe." (Rom. iv:11.) "They which be of faith, are blessed with faithful Abraham." The unbelieving and unholy are impartially excluded; for "if any man have not the Spirit of Christ, he is none of his." "He that believeth not the Son, shall not see life; but the wrath of God abideth on him." (John iii:36.) Now, since our passage does not teach that the seed of Abraham includes all mankind, it is therefore no proof of universal salvation. Nor is it any link in the chain of such proof unless other passages prove that all mankind will finally possess faith and holiness. No such passages can be found; but, could they be, then the passage under consideration would no longer be needed as proof of universal salvation.

3. It has also been inferred that, since Jesus will "destroy him that hath the power of death, that is the devil," therefore all men without exception, will be saved.

Should we take "destroy" to mean "annihilate" the passage even then would not teach the final salvation of all men; since there is no certain connection between Satan's annihilation, and the holiness of all those whom he has led into sin. The original mutineer may be killed, and yet others persist in the mutiny. Or, for all that our passage teaches to the contrary, both the devil and those who are of their father, the devil (John viii:44), may together be destroyed.

But the passage does not teach the annihilation of the devil. The original word translated "destroy" means "to render ineffective," "deprive of efficacy." Now, it was for the sake of "the children" that Jesus partook of flesh and blood, and, so far as is necessary to effect the deliverance of the children, our passage does teach that Christ will "render ineffective" the devil, but no further. When a man of war renders a pirate captain ineffective by putting him into chains, it is not at all a necessary consequence that his willing crew go free; rather do captain and crew go together into chains.

I John iv:8: "God is love." From the fact that God is love, together with the fact of his infinite power, the final salvation of all men has been inferred. That this inference is correct, no mortal man is able to prove. If correct, it is reasonable to think that Christ, the divine teacher, who gave the great proof of God's love, or John who asserts that God is love, would have sanctioned it. Yet neither Christ, nor any New Testament writer, gives it his sanction. This absence of sanction by teachers sent of God, certainly gives rise to reasonable doubt of its correctness. The argument from the love of God is employed with great frequency by every Universalist preacher, and great reliance is evidently placed upon it; yet throughout the whole New Testament—that revelation which is affirmed to have been given for the very purpose of teaching the final salvation of every man—the argument is not even once employed. How account for this omission? Did Christ but half perform his duty? *Yes, if Universalists are right.* The statement of Christ that God is love, and therefore all mankind, without exception, will finally be saved—together with the omission of certain orthodox arguments, would have made the Church of Christ Universalist in doctrine beyond all earthly power of hindrance. The resurrected Christ who spake to the sad disciples till their hearts burned within them by the way,—the ascended Christ who poured on the praying disciples the Pentecostal baptism of the Holy Ghost and fire,—the glorified Christ who sat down at "the right hand of the Majesty on high," and to whom all power in earth and heaven was given, could doubtless with prophetic vision distinctly trace the course on earth of his historical and blood-bought church. He knew that for seventeen or eighteen centuries every branch of that historical church—that faithful church which bore aloft through seas of blood the banner of the crucified, would reject as unscriptural and untrue the doctrine of universal salvation. By the lifting of a finger—by the speaking of a sentence—by a single volition, he could have written within and without on the walls of that church—on its doors and windows—on its pulpit and pews—on its foundation and its top stone, the sentence: "God is love, and therefore all mankind, without exception, will finally be saved." But he did not. And why? Because he did not prize as highly the character of God, or the welfare of man as Universalist preachers?

No, but it is reasonable to believe, because the inference which that sentence contains, is unsound and false. Such a statement, if true, would certainly have shown on the part of Christ benevolence and love which would have gladdened the hearts of universal humanity, as no recorded statement of his has done. Now brother fears for brother, parent fears for child, and friend fears for friend. Now the tear starts in secret, and dying ones moan in agony. And the words of Christ have helped to make it so. To millions of thoughtful men who recognize in Christ a divine teacher, yet have not yielded to his claims, his words are often words of terror. Yea, how often has the sincere Christian, perhaps through causes beyond his control, passed hours of anxious thought, lest after all he has built for eternity, not on the rock, but on shifting sand, and in vain. Jesus has so shaped his teachings as to make probably ninety-nine out of every hundred believers in Christianity understand him to teach the doctrine of everlasting condemnation. Now, if he was sent of God, as Universalists affirm, to teach the doctrine of universal salvation, it necessarily follows, either that he knew not how to convey his ideas by language, or that he was wilfully disobedient to

God. But since neither of these alternatives is true, it follows of necessity that he was not sent of God to teach the doctrine of universal salvation. And therefore neither did he himself, nor any disciple write on the page of inspiration the sentence : "God is love, and therefore all mankind will finally be saved."

2. The argument proves too much. It affirms that all men will finally be saved because they are creatures of God, who is love. Everything needed for their final happiness God will make sure. He does not save men because they comply with conditions prescribed,—because they are penitent for sin,—because they believe in Christ. He saves all men, notwithstanding all possible wickedness, because He is love. In short, no man can be so wicked as to avoid final salvation. The mercenary midnight assassin—the bloody murderers of the innocents at Bethlehem—the treacherous Judas—is just as sure to shine in endless glory as Paul, or John, or Christ. "So far as admission to endless glory is concerned, the saint and sinner stand on a perfect level." (O. A. Skinner.)

"Do you ask me in what I trust the salvation of (all) men? It is what you or I or anybody can trust. It is an infinite love which can pardon according to the measure of our sins, a love which will reach far beyond our wickedness." (E. H. Chapin.)

Moses tells us that "God saw everything that He had made, and behold it was very good." The Psalmist that "His tender mercies are over all his works." Now since God is love, and is infinite, He is love not to man alone (that would make him partial), but to all his sentient creation. And therefore if the fact that he is love makes the final salvation of all men certain, it also makes the final salvation of all serpents, grizzly bears, and mosquitoes, certain. The argument is based neither on God's promise nor man's desert; neither on moral or intellectual faculty in man, but on love in God. And therefore if that love, being infinite and impartial, will avail for man it will avail for monkey, and for all sentient creation; since these sustain as really as man the relation of creature to a God of love. Jonah may repeat his unique three days' voyage in his animated submarine boat; Du Chaillu may inform Gorilla that his shooting was for curiosity and fame, and not for any special dislike; and Gorilla may express his hearty satisfaction for his, though somewhat painful, yet speedy removal from a troublous world to the abodes of endless glory, where berries are plenty and hunters are scarce. Yet who knows but what Du Chaillu and the Western hunters who were too much for Grizzly, may have, in a land where guns and ammunition are no more, just a little suspicion that the disposition of their old foes may not have been even by the resurrection made utterly lamb-like,—may feel that it is not exactly safe to come within the sweep of those huge paws, lest by some possibility the old animosity might suddenly revive. It is indeed asserted in Scripture that "the wolf and the lamb shall feed together, and the lion shall eat straw like the bullock, and dust shall be the serpent's meat. They shall not hurt nor destroy in all my holy mountain, saith the Lord." (Isa. lxv:25.)

But if we should admit that this passage relates to all sentient beings, who can certify us that it has any relation whatever to a life beyond the grave; that it is not an interpolation; or if that be improbable, that the prophet being at the time of writing perhaps not fully under the influence of the inspiring spirit, may not have been somewhat mistaken. But whatever this or similar passages may mean, let us have no partiality in God. And, if the argument be sound, that all men, because they are creatures of a God of love, will finally be saved, let that same argument be considered sufficient to prove the final salvation of all the fierce inhabitants of earth and air and sea. But since this strictly logical conclusion is in the absence of positive revelation to that effect, untenable ; therefore, the argument which conducts to such conclusion, is also untenable.

3. The argument is based on an erroneous supposition. It takes for granted that the conduct of an infinite Being possessing a certain attribute, can be determined with certainty by the conduct of a finite being possessing the same attribute. And since an earthly parent loving his child would not (were it possible to avoid it) allow him to sin and suffer perpetually, therefore God who is love and is omnipotent, will not allow any being whom he has created to sin and suffer perpetually. Thus certain knowledge of the finite is affirmed to conduct to certain knowledge of the Infinite. A position impossible to be sustained, since the relation between the finite and the infinite cannot be understood by man. The folly of attempting to reason from the finite to the infinite is easily shown. An earthly parent wise, loving, and of sufficient power, would not allow a child to fall into habits of life such as would of neces-

sity bring after them life-long suffering. Now if we can reason with certainty from the conduct of the finite to the conduct of the infinite, then God who is wise and loving and of sufficient power, does not allow any of his children by creation to fall into habits such as necessitate lifelong suffering. But undeniable facts show that God does allow his children by creation to fall into such habits. Some learn to love the intoxicating cup, some are trained to theft, profanity and impurity; the intellectual and moral condition of whole nations is low and degraded; "The dark places of the earth are full of the habitations of cruelty," yet God allows it all, and has for generations. Now since the infinite God of love does in one instance what the finite loving parent would not do, therefore in other instances—and in the matter of endless sin and suffering—infinite love may do what finite love would not do. There is philosophy as well as piety in Paul's exclamation—"How unsearchable are his judgments, and his ways past finding out!"

In closing our remarks on the argument from the love of God we offer the following syllogism:

Major. Every father who is able to make his children as holy and happy without subjecting them to crime and wretchedness as by so subjecting them, is a cruel father if he subject them to crime and wretchedness.

Minor. The Father, God, who is able to make his children just as holy and happy without subjecting them to crime and wretchedness as by so subjecting them, does subject his children to crime and wretchedness.

Conclusion. Therefore, the Father, God, is a cruel Father.

Now it is impossible to deny the truthfulness of this conclusion without also denying the truthfulness of one of the premises. But since this conclusion is contrary to the first principles of Christianity, therefore the truthfulness of one of the premises must be denied. Of which one? Not of the minor, for both fact and Scripture teach us that, notwithstanding God's omnipotence, his human children are made subject to crime and wretchedness.

The major premise, then, must be in fault. What is that fault? It is in asserting that to be true of the divine and infinite Father which can only be truthfully asserted of finite fathers. Now Universalism either does or does not assert that the action of the infinite Father toward his children, can be determ ined by the action of finite fathers toward their children. If it does not, then it yields the argument from the Fatherhood of God. If it does, then it must accept as correct the conclusion that God is a cruel Father. But since no Christian can accept such a conclusion as correct, therefore it is impossible to determine from the action of a finite father what will be the action of the infinite Father.

Rev. xxi:3, 4: "The Tabernacle of God is with men, and he will dwell with them, and they shall be his people, and God himself shall be with them, and be their God. And God shall wipe away all tears from their eyes; and there shall be no more death, neither sorrow nor crying, neither shall there be any more pain, for the former things are passed away."

That the blessings here promised do not relate to all mankind without exception, the 7th and 8th verses of the same chapter clearly show. Those who approve themselves unto God shall experience the blessings; while the fearful, the unbelieving, etc., "shall have their part in the lake which burneth with fire and brimstone, which is the second death." And yet further the 15th verse of the 22d chapter clearly teaches that without the "holy city" are specified classes of mankind which certainly are not saved.

The passages of Scripture which have just been examined fail, we believe, to prove the doctrine of universal salvation. And that they do so fail, we further believe, every person of discrimination and candor may readily perceive. Neither do we know, nor do we think our doctrinal opponents know any passage of greater force as proofs of universal salvation than these which have just been considered. And here we might cease investigation, and consider our proposition as proved. Because, as we have shown, men, after the judgment, are in a state of condemnation; because no man escapes from condemnation but by Christ; and, because the passages we have examined, and there are no stronger, fail to prove that Christ will bring all men without exception, out of condemnation into reconciliation and favor.

But since the Scriptures not only refrain from asserting the restoration of all mankind, but do also positively assert the endless condemnation of those who through life reject Christ, we shall also notice some of those positive teachings.

And as having a bearing on the endless condemnation of the wicked, since it throws light on the nature of the penalty of sin, we present first; I Cor. xv:22. "For as in Adam all die, even so in Christ shall all be made alive."

Both parties affirm that the being "made alive" in Christ here spoken, is a life which is endless. But if the life in Christ is endless it follows of necessity that the death in Adam is also endless. We do not mean to affirm that those who die in Adam will never be released from endless death, for, through God's grace, a multitude which no man can number will be released from that death; but, that the penalty of death in Adam is, in its nature, endless. A criminal sentenced to die, may by pardon escape the death, yet the escaping through pardon does not in the least degree change the nature of the penalty. So, even though a great multitude escape the penalty of endless death, that does not in the slightest degree change the nature of the penalty.

Our thoughts on this passage will take the form of question and answer, as follows:

1. When Paul says, "As in Adam all die, even so in Christ shall all be made alive,' does the life to which he refers contain the idea of endlessness? Ans. Yes.

2. Is not the life in Christ a deliverance from the death in Adam? Ans. Yes.

3. When a prisoner is sentenced for two

years, can the Governor, accurately speaking, pardon him for ten years? Ans. No.

4. When the deliverance comes not by expiration of the time of imprisonment but by gracious pardon, does not the duration of the deliverance exactly correspond with the duration of the unexpired time of imprisonment? Ans. Yes.

5. Does the deliverance which Christ's people experience come by expiration of time of imprisonment, or, by gracious pardon? Ans. By gracious pardon.

6. Since the duration of a deliverance by gracious pardon exactly corresponds with the duration of the unexpired time of imprisonment; and since the deliverance which Christ's people experience comes by gracious pardon, does not the deliverance which Christ's people experience exactly correspond with the duration of the unexpired time of imprisonment? Ans. Yes.

7. Since the deliverance which Christ's people experience exactly corresponds with the duration of the unexpired time of imprisonment, and since the deliverance which Christ's people experience is endless, is not the duration of the unexpired time of imprisonment also endless? Ans. Yes.

Now since the death in Adam is in its

nature an endless death it follows of necessity that if any of Adam's race are not rescued, they must die endlessly.

Another passage which throws light on the nature of the penalty of sin is Rom. vi:23: "The wages of sin is death, but the gift of God is eternal life through Jesus Christ, our Lord." The life here spoken of while spiritual, is still endless. It may and does begin this side of the grave, but it also lasts forever beyond the grave; as is plainly proved by the following statements of Jesus: "Labor not for the meat that perisheth, but for that meat which endureth unto everlasting life, which the Son of man shall give unto you." (Jno. vi:27). "And this is the will of Him that sent me that every one which seeth the Son and believeth on him may have everlasting life; and I will raise him up at the last day." (Jno. vi:40). "This is the bread which cometh down from heaven that a man may eat thereof and not die. 1 am the living bread which came down from heaven. If any man eat of this bread he shall live forever." "Whoso eateth my flesh and drinketh my blood, hath eternal life; and I will raise him up at the last day." (Jno. vi: 50, 51, 54.) Here Christ connects with eternal life, not dying—living forever—being raised up at the last day, and in such a manner as clearly to teach that the eternal life which he bestows is endless in its duration. Now should this endless life not be secured, what remains of necessity for him who fails to secure it, but endless death? Is it possible that intelligent men can fail to see that whoever does not obtain a gift is of necessity destitute of that gift, whatever it may be?

If a child in a family—a pupil in a school—a citizen in a state, does not receive a certain gift, what can be plainer than that he is necessarily destitute of it?

And surely there can be nothing in the mere fact that a gift comes from God to reverse a necessity, and make that one who does not obtain a certain gift, does yet possess that same gift. Now since the gift which comes from God is endless life, it necessarily follows that whosoever does not receive the gift, is destitute of endless life. And whosoever is destitute of endless life must have its opposite, which is endless death. But the opposite of the gift of endless life, is the wages of sin, and therefore the wages of sin is endless death.

Rom. vi:21, 22, "What fruit had ye then in those things whereof ye are now ashamed? for the end of those things is death.

"But now being made free from sin, and become servants to God, ye have your fruit unto holiness, and the end everlasting life."

Here two ends are mentioned. The end of things sinful, which is death; and the end of things obedient and holy, which is everlasting life.

Now since these ends are ends of opposite courses of conduct, it is very plain that the ends themselves are opposites. And therefore since the end of the one course is everlasting, that is, endless life: the end of the other course must be endless death. And further, since the endless life pertains not to the holy things done, but to the doers of them; so in like manner the endless death pertains not to the sinful things done, but to the doers of them.

The penalty, then, of sin is in its nature endless. Let us now notice the teaching of Scripture that some of mankind, through wilful rejection of Christ, will not be rescued from the penalty, but will experience it in its endlessness, just as really as others will experience the life which is the gift of God in its endlessness. Gal. v:2. "Behold I Paul say unto you that if ye be circumcised, Christ shall profit you nothing."

This language, while literal and strongly

emphatic, is yet conditional. And the condition we may reasonably suppose is not the mere fact of circumcision, since Timothy was circumcised by consent of Paul, but submission to that rite for the purpose of being justified in the sight of God. That Paul meant the rite as used for this purpose is also shown by the fourth verse, "Christ is become of none effect unto you whosoever of you are justified by the law ; ye are fallen from grace."

Now since the gospel teaches that justification before God is obtained alone through faith in Christ, it follows that whosoever seeks justification in any other way than through faith in Christ, is governed in his conduct by principles hostile to the gospel of Christ. And because of such hostility of principle the apostle uses the strong language, "Behold, I Paul, say unto you that, if ye be circumcised, Christ shall profit you nothing."

The question now arises, Did any fulfil the condition? And on this question the history of the church throws light. Mosheim says (Bk. I, Cent. II, Part II, Ch v.), "This body of people who would unite Moses and Christ, was again divided into two classes, differing widely in their opinions and customs, the *Nazareans* and the *Ebionites*. The former are not reckoned by the ancient Christians among heretics; but the latter are placed among the sects which subverted the foundations of religion. * * * Whether the Ebionites derived their name from a man [called *Ebion*], or were so denominated on account of their *poverty*, either in regard to property or sentiment, is uncertain. But they were much worse than the Nazareans. For though they supposed *Christ* to be an ambassador of God and endowed with divine power, yet they conceived him to be a man, born in the ordinary course of nature, the son of *Joseph* and *Mary*. They maintained that the ceremonial law of *Moses* must be observed, not by the Jews only, but by all who wished to obtain salvation; and therefore *St. Paul*, that strenuous opposer of the law, they viewed with abhorrence."

Neander says (Hist. of Chris. Rel. and Church), Vol. I, 342, 343): "About the middle of the second century we still find among the Christians of Jewish descent, the two parties which existed in the apostolic age. This is evident from a passage in the dialogue of Justin Martyr with Trypho. Two classes are here mentioned,—they who in their own practice united with the faith in Christ the observance of the Mosaic law, but without requiring the same observance of believing pagans, whom they acknowledged rather as genuine Christian brethren, and accounted worthy of all brotherly fellowship, notwithstanding that they maintained their original Christian freedom—and they who were not content with observing the Mosaic law themselves, but were for forcing the pagan believers universally to the same observance, and who refused otherwise to have fellowship with them; thus proceeding on the assumption that the *believing* pagans, like all others, were *unclean*, and that without the observance of the Mosaic law no man could be just before God. The former were the genuinely apostolic Jewish Christians, who had remained true to the pledge of agreement made at Jerusalem; the latter belonged to that party with whose influence the apostle Paul has so often to struggle among the communities of pagan Christians."

These historical extracts plainly show that some did fulfil the condition; since it would be absurd to suppose that earnest Pharasaic Jews would labor for generations among nominal Christians, and yet succeed in making no perverts. It is true then of some that Christ shall profit them nothing. Now since the penalty of sin is endless death, and since no sinner can be saved but by Christ; and since Christ shall profit these sinners spoken of, nothing, therefore, these sinners shall never be released from the penalty of endless death.

II Cor. xi:14, 15: "Satan fashioneth himself into an angel of light. Therefore it is no great thing if his ministers also fashion themselves as ministers of righteousness, whose end shall be according to their works." (Rev. Ver.)

This passage is not presented in proof of future punishment to one who denies it, but in proof of the endlessness of future punishment to one who believes in future punishment, but denies its endlessness. Now, since a Restorationist (with whom alone we are now arguing) admits the doctrine of punishment beyond the grave, he must also, from that very fact, admit that the end of these wicked ones is experienced beyond the grave. For if their end, in accordance with their wickedness, is experienced altogether in this life, there can be no punishment subsequent to this life. Now, the *end* of these is their final state. And since their final state is to be in accordance with works of wickedness, that final state must be one of condemnation. And since there is no state beyond the final, that condemnation is never escaped from. In other words, it is endless.

I Pet.iv:17 : "For the time is come that judgment must begin at the house of God. And if it first begin at us, what shall the end be of them that obey not the gospel of God?"

Two classes of persons are here spoken of, sincere Christians, and those who live and die in disobedience. Their disobedience is the crime—their end is the penalty for their crime, and is therefore of necessity something different from, and subsequent to, their crime. And as their crime continued till their death, and as the penalty of crime is subsequent to crime, therefore their end—their penalty—is subsequent to their death. The end, then, of which the apostle speaks, is experienced, by the disobedient, in the life beyond the grave. And of course, the end, of good or bad, in the life beyond the grave, is their final condition. Now it is as plainly to be seen as the earth in daylight, that the apostle is speaking of the penalty of wickedness—is giving a warning—and a warning is given not concerning a good, but an evil. Therefore the final condition of the disobedient, in the life beyond the grave, is an evil condition.

Phil. iii:18, 19 : " For many walk of whom I have told you often, and now tell you even weeping, that they are the enemies of the cross of Christ. Whose end is destruction, whose god is their belly, and whose glory is in their shame, who mind earthly things."

Whatever the apostle here means by "end" (*telos*), it is very plain that he does not mean anything which pertains alike to both the friends and the enemies of the cross, but that which pertains to enemies alone. He is exhorting his hearers to faith and holiness; he is dissuading them from unbelief and sin. And to influence them, he tells of the blessings of the one course, and of the evils of the other. And therefore the mentioning as a motive of anything to be unavoidably experienced by both parties, is manifestly out of place. Therefore by "end" he does not mean physical death, whether painful or otherwise, since that is experienced by both friends and foes of the cross. It is also evident that "end" (*telos*) is not to be understood in the sense of "purpose;" since such meaning is inconsistent with the character of the god whom these enemies worshiped, and of the things on which their hearts were set.

Nor does the context indicate that the tears of the apostle flowed for the sorrow to be endured on earth by these enemies of the cross. His description of them forbids the idea that they would be greatly troubled by moral considerations, and with persecution for the cause of Christ they would not, of course, be troubled. Nor can Restorationists, since they admit punishment in a future state, claim that the suffering over which Paul wept is confined to earth, but must admit that it is experienced in a future state of existence. The "end" (*telos*), then, is experienced beyond the grave. Remembering this fact, give now to "end" (*telos*) its ordinary meaning—termination—completion—issue—which alone the context allows, and then Paul says: "Enemies of the cross of Christ, whose issue or termination or completion, is destruction." And, of course, if their termination beyond the grave be destruction, it cannot also be salvation.

I Tim. vi:9: "But they that will be rich, fall into temptation, and a snare, and into many foolish and hurtful lusts, which drown men in destruction and perdition."

Since not alone in the apostles' time, but in every century since, there have been men determined at all hazards to be rich, we presume that no Restorationist will question the fact that the perdition of which the apostle speaks is actually experienced by men.

Paul teaches the same fact also, when he says (Heb. x:39): "We are not of them who draw back unto perdition, but of them that believe to the saving of the soul."

Christ also teaches the same in John xvii:12: " None of them is lost but the son of perdition ;" and in Matt. vii:13, 14 : " Broad is the way that leadeth to destruction (or perdition) and many there be which go in thereat * * * narrow is the way that leadeth unto life, and few there be that find it."

Those who do not find the way of life, of course, experience the perdition of which Christ speaks.

The word in question is, in the original Greek, *apoleiá*. Let us now endeavor to ascertain its meaning by noticing the passages of Scripture in which it occurs.

The disciples used the word when they said (Matt. xxvi:8, 9): " To what purpose is this *waste?* (*Apoleia.*) For this ointment might have been sold for much, and given to the poor;" and, as used by them, it clearly excludes all idea of a recovery, since the ointment once used was gone forever.

The word in Mark. xiv:4, has the same idea of finality.

In Acts viii:20, Peter said to Simon : " Thy money perish—be to perdition, *apoleia*—with thee." Peter certainly did not mean to say, Lay it aside and I will take it by and by.

In Acts xxv:16, Festus said : " It is not the custom of the Romans to deliver any man to die—to perdition, *apoleia*—before that he which is accused, have the accusers face to face."

Here the *apoleia*—perdition—means death, and of course has the idea of finality, since the Romans knew nothing of a physical resurrection.

In Rom. ix:23, Paul speaks of " vessels of wrath fitted to destruction—*apoleia*—and vessels of mercy prepared unto glory;" and since the vessels of wrath are different from the vessels of glory, and since the glory of the vessels of mercy is final, therefore the destruction of the vessels of wrath is also final.

In Phil. i:28, Paul says: " And in nothing terrified by your adversaries, which is to them an evident token of perdition (*apoleia*), but to you of salvation, and that of God." Here certainly no hint is given that the perdition is not final.

Phil. iii:18, 19: "Enemies of the cross of Christ, whose end is destruction (*apoleia*)." Here, very plainly, the destruction is final.

II Thess. ii:3, 4 : " Let no man deceive you by any means, for that day shall not come except there come a falling away first, and that man of sin be revealed, the son of perdition (*apoleia*), who opposeth and exalteth himself above all that is called God." Here, very plainly, the perdition is final.

I Tim. vi:9: "But they that will be rich, fall into temptation and a snare, and into many foolish and hurtful lusts, which drown men in destruction and perdition (*apoleia*)." Here the word contains no idea of a restoration.

Heb. x:39: "But we are not of them who draw back unto perdition (apoleia), but of them that believe to the saving of the soul." Here the word contains no idea of a restoration. And if the doctrine of Restoration be true, those who drew back unto perdition, could have said to Paul and his believing companions: "We shall just as certainly be saved as you."

II Peter ii:1: "False teachers among you who privily shall bring in damnable heresies (literally, heresies of perdition) (*apoleia*); even denying the Lord that bought them, and bring upon themselves swift destruction" (apoleia.)

Since God uses true faith, not heresies to conduct men to salvation, and since it is unscriptural to assert the denial of the Lord will bring swift restoration, therefore the word *apoleia* as here used, contains no idea of a restoration.

II Peter ii:2 : " And many shall follow their pernicious ways (literally their perditions, *apoleia*), by reason of whom the way of truth shall be evil spoken of." Here certainly the word contains no idea of restoration.

II Peter ii:3 : " Whose judgment now of a long time lingereth not, and their damnation (*apoleia*) slumbereth not." As here used, the word contains no idea of a restoration.

II Peter iii:7 : "But the heavens and earth which are now by the same word kept in store, reserved unto fire against the day of judgment and perdition *apoleia* of ungodly men."

The word, here, suggests no idea of a restoration.

II Peter iii:16 : "In which (epistles) are some things hard to be understood, which they that are unlearned and unstable, wrest, as they do also the other Scriptures, unto their own destruction *apoleia*. The context indicates that the perdition is final, since it compares their fate to the fate of beasts, saying (ii:12) : "But these as natural brute beasts, made to be taken and destroyed, speak evil of the things that they understand not, and shall utterly perish in their own corruption."

Matt. vii:13, 14 : "Enter ye in at the strait gate, for wide is the gate, and broad is the way that leads to destruction (*apoleia*), and many there be which go in thereat. Because strait is the gate, and narrow is the way which leadeth unto life, and few there be that find it." Here, since the force of Christ's reasoning depends upon it, the perdition is final. Yet, according to Restorationism, Christ at the very moment of uttering the statement, knew in his heart that every son of perdition, without exception, would find and enjoy the endless and blessed life by and by. According to Restorationism, Christ means to say: "Enter ye in at the strait gate; for wide is the gate, and broad is the way that leadeth to *ultimate restoration*, and many there be which go in thereat. Because strait is the gate, and narrow is the way, which leadeth unto life, and few there be that find it."

Or, in other words, "Don't go the roundabout way to heaven; but take the direct road." And if such was his meaning, how singular his choice of words to express that meaning.

Rev. xvii:8 : The beast that thou sawest, was, and is not; and shall ascend out of the bottomless pit, and go into perdition," *apoleia*.

Rev. xvii:11: "And the beast that was, and is not, even he is the eighth, and is of the seven, and goeth into perdition" (*apoleia*). Surely the scarlet-colored beast, full of the names of blasphemy, when he goes into perdition, does not by that very perdition experience a process of restoration. The context also indicates the finality of the perdition, since it says (xx:10): "And the devil that deceived them, was cast into the lake of fire and brimstone, where the beast and the false prophet are, and shall be tormented day and night, forever and ever." The original words translated "forever and ever," are frequently used in ascriptions of praise to God, as follows: Gal. i:5: "To whom be glory forever and ever;" Phil. iv:20: "Now unto God and our Father be glory forever and ever;" I Tim. i:17: "Now unto the King eternal, immortal, invisible, the only wise God, be honor and glory forever and ever;" and do therefore contain the idea of endless duration.

We have now noticed every passage in the New Testament, where *apoleia* occurs.

And as a result of our investigation, we see that the Scriptural meaning of *apoleia* is a perdition with no idea of a restoration.

But, as has already been shown from

Scripture, some of mankind experience this perdition, and therefore the doctrine of universal restoration is untrue.

And here though we have used the words *aion*, meaning an age, or eternity, and *aionios*, meaning everlasting, eternal; only in an indirect way (as proving the endless salvation of believers, and the endless torment of the devil, the beast, and the false prophet, without asserting who these are), we might safely, with no further proof, consider our position as sustained. Yet since these words do have a bearing on the question, we notice them.

In reference to *aion* we make the two following statements, which, if correct, do overthrow the doctrine of final restoration.

First:—The word *aion* as used in the New Testament in the phrase *eis ton aiona*, always, without an exception, indicates an endless duration.

Second.—The word *aion* as used in the phrase *eis ton aiona*, is employed in the New Testament to indicate the duration of the condemnation of certain wicked ones.

In proof of our first statement we invite attention to the following passages of Scripture in which the phrase occurs.

Matt. xxi:19: "Christ said unto the fig

tree: "Let no fruit grow on thee henceforward forever."

Mark xi:14: "Jesus said unto the fig tree: "No man eat fruit of thee hereafter forever."

Luke i:55: "As he spake to our fathers, to Abraham and to his seed forever."

John iv:14: "But whosoever drinketh of the water that I shall give him, shall never thirst."

John vi:51: "If any man eat of this bread, he shall live forever."

John vi:58: "He that eateth of this bread, shall live forever."

John viii:35, 51, 52: "And the servant abideth not in the house forever; but the son abideth ever." "If a man keep my saying he shall never see death." Verse 52 is the same as 51 (so far as the phrase is concerned).

John x:28: "And I give unto them eternal life, and they shall never perish."

John xi:26: "And whosoever liveth and believeth in me, shall never die."

John xii:34: "We have heard out of the law, that Christ abideth forever."

John xiii:8: "Peter saith unto him, Thou shalt never wash my feet."

John xiv:16: "And I will pray the Father, and he shall give you another Comforter, that he may abide with you forever."

I Cor. viii:13: "If meat make my brother to offend, I will eat no flesh while the world standeth" (literally forever).

II Cor. ix:9: "His righteousness remaineth forever."

Heb. v:6: "Thou art a priest forever after the order of Melchizedek."

Heb. vi:20: "Jesus made a high priest forever, after the order of Melchizedek."

Heb. vii:17 and vii:21 are both the same as vi:20.

Heb. vii:24: "But this man, because he continueth forever, hath an unchangeable priesthood."

Heb. vii:28: "For the law maketh men high priests, which have infirmity; but the word of the oath which was since the law, maketh the Son who is consecrated forevermore."

I Peter i:23: "The word of God which liveth and abideth forever."

I Peter i:25: "The word of the Lord endureth forever."

I John ii:17: "He that doeth the will of God, abideth forever."

II. John ii: "For the truth sake, which dwelleth in us, and shall be with us forever." The phrase "*eis ton aiona*" in all these passages clearly signifies an endless duration.

Now, there are but two other passages in the New Testament in which the phrase occurs. And since both parties claim these two passages, the one party as not being opposed by them, the other party as being supported by them, therefore the meaning of the phrase must be determined without at all consulting the two passages. But without consulting the two passages the meaning of the phrase *"eis ton aiona"* is an endless duration, as has just been shown.

We may now legitimately apply its ascertained meaning to the two disputed passages. One occurs in Mark iii:29, thus: " But he that shall blaspheme against the Holy Ghost, hath never forgiveness" (literally hath not forgiveness forever, or for the endless duration). The other occurs in Jude xiii: "Wandering stars to whom is reserved the blackness of darkness forever—*eis ton aiona*—for the endless duration." Should the divine authority of Jude be denied, that of Mark still remains, and then instead of some twenty-six undisputed passages determining the meaning of two disputed ones, those twenty-six passages determine the meaning of but one disputed passage. And that the blasphemy against the Holy Ghost referred to by Mark, was actually committed, Universalist divines themselves affirm. Rev. T. J. Sawyer, D.D., says (Discussion on Eternal Salvation, pp. 174 and 175): "The blasphemy against the Holy Spirit is the *only* exception. If we can find what *that* sin was, we know how far we can go and escape endless damnation. By the Bible you will see that the Jews sinned in this way, because they ascribed the miracles of Christ to Beelzebub."

Rev. J. M. Austin says (Debate on Endless Punishment, p. 702): " What is the sin against the Holy Ghost? It consisted in ascribing the *power* by which Jesus performed his miracles, to an imaginary evil spirit—to *Beelzebub*, an idol which the heathen Ekronites worshiped as "the god of flies"—instead of ascribing it to God. * * * Thus the sin was peculiarly a *Jewish* one. It was also a *national* sin. It was committed alone by those in whose midst Jesus performed his miracles." The sin then was actually committed, and thus our second statement is shown to be correct. That statement is— that *aion* as used in the phrase *"eis ton aiona,"* is employed in the New Testament to indicate the duration of the condemnation of certain wicked ones. And since *aion* as used in that phrase, indicates, without an exception, an endless duration, therefore the condemnation of certain wicked ones, is an endless condemnation.

Respecting *aionios* we have three statements to make, the correctness of which we shall endeavor to show as they are successively announced.

First, the general, if not universal, meaning of *aionios*, as used in the New Testament, is endless duration. In proof of this the following facts are offered:

1. *Aionios* is used to indicate the duration of God's existence. Rom. xvi:26. "According to the commandment of the everlasting (*aionios*) God."

2. *Aionios* is used to indicate the duration of the Spirit of God. Heb. ix:14, "Christ, who, through the eternal (*aionios*) Spirit offered himself without spot to God."

3. *Aionios* is used to indicate the duration of the glory of God. I Peter v:10, "The God of all grace who hath called us unto his eternal (*aionios*) glory."

4. *Aionios* is used to indicate the duration of the honor and power ascribed to the King of kings. I Tim. vi:15, 16, "The King of kings, and Lord of Lords, who only hath immortality, dwelling in the light which no man can approach unto; whom no man hath seen nor can see; to whom be honor and power everlasting." (*Aionios*).

5. *Aionios* is used as an equivalent to *aion* of the phrase *eis ton aiona* in which as has been shown, *aion* means an endless duration. Mark iii:29. "He that shall blaspheme against the Holy Ghost hath never (*eis ton aiona*) forgiveness but is in danger of eternal (*aionios*) damnation."

6. *Aionios* is used to indicate the duration of the habitations of the blessed in the life beyond the grave. Luke xvi:9. "Make to yourselves friends of the mammon of unrighteousness; that when ye fail, they may receive you into everlasting (*aionios*) habitations." II Cor. v:1, "For we know, that, if our earthly house of this tabernacle were dissolved, we have a building of God, a house not made with hands, eternal (*aionios*) in the heavens."

7. *Aionios* is used to indicate an endless duration in contrast to one which is but temporary. II Cor. iv:18, "The things which are seen are temporal, but the things which are unseen are eternal (*aionios*)."

8. *Aionios* is used to indicate the duration of the redemption which Christ obtained. Heb. ix:12. "He entered in once into the holy place having obtained eternal (*aionios*) redemption."

9. *Aionios* is used to indicate the life of the finally saved. Rom. ii:7. "To them who

by patient continuance in well doing seek for glory, honor and immortality, (God will render) eternal (*aionios*) life." Rom. v:21, "That as sin hath reigned unto death, even so might grace reign through righteousness unto eternal (*aionios*) life, by Jesus Christ our Lord." Rom. vi:23, "For the wages of sin is death, but the gift of God is eternal (*aionios*) life, through Jesus Christ, our Lord." Jno. xvii:2. "Thou hast given him power over all flesh that he should give eternal (*aionios*) life to as many as thou hast given him."

These instances, which might easily be made more numerous, are fully sufficient to show the correctness of our first statement; that the general meaning of *aionios*, as used in the New Testament, is an endless duration. It is simply impossible for any Restorationist to select from the New Testament a list of subjects so various or of instances so numerous as has just been given, to which *aionios*, as signifying a limited duration, is applied. Indeed, though the word occurs some seventy times in the New Testament, we think it would be difficult to present proof sufficient to secure a reasonable belief that the word is used in the sense of a limited duration, more than three times out of the seventy.

On this point Prof. Alex. McClelland says,

(Canon and Interpretation of the Scriptures p. 147): "The adjective *aionios*, is commonly used by the Greeks for 'eternal' or 'everlasting,' and is the strongest term they can employ; in this sense it is constantly used in the New Testament, with perhaps one or two exceptions."

Our second statement is, thus: When *aionios* is applied to anything, which is not, from any source, known to be of limited duration, then *aionios* must be considered to have its usual meaning of endless duration.

This statement is but the application to *aionios* of the universally acknowledged principle that, when no cause exists to the contrary, words must be understood to have their ordinary meaning. Take an illustration or two of this very plain principle. Our friend Mr. A, borrows of his Restorationist friend Mr. B, just for a single day, his splendid carriage and horses.

Now fancy if you can the feelings of Mr. B when his friend coolly informs him that the single day for which the carriage and horses were borrowed is to be understood in the sense of a geological day (of some thousands of years) and that when that geological day draws to a close, he will endeavor to return the borrowed articles.

Again, on the strength of Mr. A's representation that he is the owner, free of debt, of some fifteen houses in New York City, Mr. B. loans him ten thousand dollars. Fancy now, the rising indignation of Mr. B. on learning that the fifteen houses in New York City are toy houses, and might all be carried on the arm of a child.

Should a government promise its disabled soldiers lifelong assistance, and then afterward say, "Yes, lifelong assistance was promised, but the lifelong is to be understood as meaning the life duration of an ephemera," what a juggling with words and promises this would be.

Aionios, then, like all other words, is always to be understood in its usual meaning of endless duration unless there is sufficient cause for understanding it in the unusual meaning of limited duration. But the only reason which any one gives why it should be thought to mean a limited duration is the temporary nature of the thing to which it is applied. On this point Rev. J. M. Austin says (Debate on Endless Punishment, p. 746), "I have repeatedly defined my position to be that, when applied to punishment, and other things which from their nature are temporary, then *aionios* signifies a limited duration.

But that when used in reference to the Deity, his attributes, or to anything connected with an immortal existence, it then conveys a meaning of strictly endless duration." Here the only reason given why *aionios* means a limited duration, is, that the thing to which it is applied is of a temporary nature. No other valid reason can be given. Now since the usual meaning of *aionios* (as was shown under the first statement) is endless duration; and since nothing but the temporary nature of the thing to which it is applied is sufficient to give it the meaning of limited duration, therefore in every case where our doctrinal opponents assert that it means but a limited duration, they are bound to show that the thing to which it is applied is of a temporary nature.

For when any word, wherever occurring, is asserted to possess an unusual meaning, he who makes the assertion, if he would be believed, is bound to give proof of its unusual meaning. And thus our second statement is shown to be correct.

The third statement is thus: The destruction of the wicked, to which in II Thess. i:9, *aionios* is applied is not from any source, known to be of a temporary nature. "Who shall be punished with everlasting destruction,"—*aionios olethros*. Besides II Thess. i:9, the word *olethros*, translated destruction, is used but three times in the New Testament, as follows: I Cor. v:5, "To deliver such an one to Satan for the destruction (*olethros*) of the flesh, that the spirit may be saved in the day of the Lord Jesus."

Did Paul say, Deliver such an one to Satan for the destruction of the flesh that the (same) flesh may be saved, then the argument would be good that *olethros* here signifies but a temporary destruction. But that which is to be saved is a different thing from that which is to be destroyed. The one is the spirit, the other is the flesh. And the salvation of the spirit is no proof of the salvation of the flesh. For Paul frequently uses the term "flesh" to signify, not material flesh, but corrupt nature; and since to understand it here in the sense of corrupt nature gives a good meaning it may here be used to signify corrupt nature. (See Rom. viii:8, 9, 13; Gal. v:17, 19, 24). And then Paul says, "To deliver such an one to Satan for the destruction of the corrupt nature, that the spirit may be saved in the day of the Lord Jesus." And our Restorationist friends certainly will not deny that, in order to have the spirit saved in the day of the Lord Jesus, the corrupt nature must be destroyed. Understood in this sense the connection is plain and even necessary, if the spirit be immortal, between the destruction of the flesh and the salvation of the spirit. But what necessary connection can be traced between the destruction of the material flesh and the salvation of the spirit?

Therefore it is impossible to prove that the destruction here spoken of is not final.

I Thess. v:3, "For when they shall say, Peace and safety, then sudden destruction (*olethros*) cometh upon them." There is nothing here to indicate that the destruction is but temporary. And the context in verse 9, by the contrast between wrath and salvation, indicates that the destruction is final.

I Tim. vi:9, "Foolish and hurtful lusts which drown men in destruction (*olethros*) and perdition." Here the destruction is final since it is associated with a perdition (*apolia*) which has already been shown (pp. 221-226) to be final.

Luke xvi:19-31. "There was a certain rich man, which was clothed in purple and fine linen, and fared sumptuously every day. And there was a certain beggar named Lazarus which was laid at his gate, full of sores, and desiring to be fed with the crumbs which fell from the rich man's table; moreover, the dogs came and licked his sores. And it came to pass that the beggar died, and was carried by the angels into Abraham's bosom. The rich man also died, and was buried; and in hell (Hades) he lifted up his eyes, being in torments, and seeth Abraham afar off, and Lazarus in his bosom. And he cried and said, Father Abraham, have mercy on me, and send Lazarus, that he may dip the tip of his finger in water, and cool my tongue ; for I am tormented in this flame. But Abraham said, Son, remember that thou in thy lifetime receivedst thy good things, and likewise Lazarus evil things; but now he is comforted, and thou art tormented. And besides all this, between us and you, there is a great gulf fixed, so that they which would pass from thence to you, cannot; neither can they pass to us, that would come from thence. Then he said, I pray thee therefore, father, that thou wouldst send him to my father's house, for I have five brethren, that he may testify unto them, lest they also come into this place of torment. Abraham saith unto him, They have Moses and the prophets; let them hear them. And he said, Nay, father Abraham; but if one went unto them from the dead, they will repent. And he said unto him, If they hear not Moses and the prophets, neither will they be persuaded, though one rose from the dead."

In the estimation of Universalists, including, we presume, Restorationists, this passage is not a history, but a parable; and its teachings, they assert, have no application to existence after physical death; but apply exclusively to events of the earthly life. Rev. T. J. Sawyer, D.D., says (Discussion on Eternal Salvation p. 177), "The rich man represented the Jewish nation. Lazarus represented the Gentiles. By their dying is meant the radical change that took place in their condition and relations, at the abolition of Judaism and the establishment of Christianity. The Gentiles were received into the kingdom of Christ, while the Jews were cast out and subjected to punishment. The great gulf expresses the relation these people now sustain to each other. During these long centuries they have not passed over from one to the other."

The following facts show that such an exposition is untenable.

1. It entirely ignores the rich man's five brothers who were yet living, and in their father's house had " Moses and the prophets."

2. It entirely ignores the best thing mentioned respecting the dead rich man, *i. e.*, his

16

desire for the enlightenment and safety of his brothers.

3. It asserts that the Jews as a nation recognize the Gentiles as enjoying, in the kingdom of the Messiah, the blissful position of faithful and accepted servants of God, which is contrary to fact.

4. It asserts that the Jews as a nation know and admit that they once possessed, and are now excluded from, the Messiah's kingdom on earth, which is contrary to fact.

5. It asserts that the Jews as a nation affirm the existence on earth of a body of their brethren, far more numerous than themselves, who are yet in possession of that kingdom of the Messiah from which they themselves have been excluded, which is contrary to fact.

6. It represents the known Jewish nation as asserting that this far more numerous body of their brethren will repent, if believing Gentiles go unto them. But it does not explain why repentance is more needful for the Jews who are in Messiah's kingdom, than for the Gentiles who are in the same kingdom.

7. It gives no meaning to about one-half of the so-called parable.

8. Paul, in Rom. xi:26, says, "All Israel shall be saved;" meaning by Israel, the Jews

as a nation on earth; but Abraham gives to the rich man in Hades no single word of hope.

Therefore, even though the passage be a parable, the above exposition is untenable. And if it be a parable, no tenable interpretation of it has yet been found. But assuming for the present that it is a parable, let us endeavor to ascertain its bearing on the argument. Each parable of Christ, all will admit, is designed to contain and to impart to those who understand it, some moral or religious instruction. And the question now arises, whether Christ ever allowed to enter into the composition of his parables any event out of harmony with the laws of matter or of mind; any event either impossible or unreasonable. No one will assert that Christ in order to compose his parables was compelled to make use of events either impossible or unreasonable. He was a special teacher from heaven, and the resources of two worlds were at his control. And when we join to this fact both the truthfulness of Christ's character, and his design of religious instruction, it certainly seems reasonable to believe that he will allow no incident of his parable to be out of harmony with natural or spiritual law. We do not mean to say that each event narrated in the parable actually occurred; for instance, supposing our passage to be a parable, that the beggar and the rich man were historical characters, and that the sores of the one, when laid in his wretchedness at the other's door, were licked by dogs; but that events similar to these—the fact of rich men and beggars—the fact of beggars being laid at rich men's doors—the fact of dogs licking sores of beggars in deep distress—not only may but *must* have occurred, or be considered as reasonable to occur, or Christ would never have allowed them a place in his parables. Let us now turn to the parables of Christ. Note the special events of the one relating to the sower. His going forth to sow—some seeds falling by the wayside—the fowls coming and devouring them—some falling on stony places, quickly springing up and quickly withering—some falling among thorns and being choked—others falling into good ground and bringing from thirty to an hundred fold; and each event is in perfect harmony with the actual experience of the sowers of that land. W. M. Thompson, D. D., for twenty-five years a missionary in Syria and Palestine, gives testimony on this matter as follows: " The parable about sowing has here its illustration even in its most minute details. Behold a sower *went forth* to sow. There is a nice and close adherence to actual life in this form of expression. These people have actually *come forth* all the way from June to this place. The expression implies that the sower in the days of our Saviour, lived in a hamlet, or village, as all these farmers now do; that he did not sow near his own house, or in a garden fenced or walled, for such a field does not furnish all the basis of the parable. There are neither *roads* nor thorns, nor stony places in such lots. He must go forth into the open country as these have done, where there are no fences; where the path passes through the cultivated land; where thorns grow in clumps all around; where the rocks peep out in places through the scanty soil; and where also, hard by, are patches extremely fertile. Now here we have the whole four within a dozen rods of us. Our horses are actually trampling down some seeds which have fallen by this wayside, and larks and sparrows are busy picking them up. That man with his mattock, is digging about places where the rock is too near the surface for the plow, and much that is sown there will wither away, because it has no deepness of earth. And not a few seeds have fallen among this *bellan*, and will be effectually choked by this most tangled of thorn bushes.

But a large portion, after all, falls into really good ground, and four months hence will exhibit every variety of crop, up to the richest and heaviest that ever rejoiced the heart even of an American farmer."

In reference to the yield of a hundred fold Dr. Robinson speaks thus: "I was greatly surprised when, discussing this question on the fertile plain of Esdraelon, to hear not merely the peasants, but intelligent gentlemen, who had rented the district from government, stoutly maintain that they had themselves, and that very year, reaped more than a hundred fold from part of that plain. I could not understand it until by accident it came out that they had a peculiar mode of calculation. In sowing they allow one-third of the seed for the birds, particularly the crows, which settle down upon the fields in countless flocks. Another third is supposed to be destroyed by mice and insects, and only one-third of the seed sown, actually comes to maturity. Thus a man sows three bushels, and if he reaps an hundred, it is a hundred fold, according to his mode of calculation, but according to ours it would only be thirty-three. * * * Barley and wheat are sown side by side in the same field, but the former gives a much heavier crop than the latter.

There is a kind of durrah—white maize—sown in this same region, which often returns several hundred fold. I have been assured by respectable farmers that they have gathered more than four hundred fold of this corn. * * * The supposition in the parable is history in the case of Isaac, who reaped a hundred fold in Gerar and 'in the same year.'"

Note the particulars of the parable of the tares. The good seed sown by the owner—the tares secretly sown by his enemy—the tares appearing with the fruit—the questioning of the servants—the reply of the owner—and they are all in thorough harmony with natural laws.

Note the particulars in the parable of the mustard seed. The smallness of the seed—the greatness of the plant or tree when grown—the lodging of the birds in the branches—and they are all in harmony with the laws which govern in the case.

The same harmony with the laws of nature prevails in the parable of the seed growing in secret, as recorded by Mark. The planting in the ground—the sleeping and rising of the planter night and day—the seed's unknown manner of growth—the earth's energy producing first the blade, then the ear, then the full corn in the ear, and the putting in of the sickle because the harvest has come.

The same harmony with natural law prevails in every recorded parable of Christ. From mustard seed planted he never brings an oak. From good seed sown he never brings tares. From tares sown by an enemy he never produces wheat. Leaven hid in meal does not turn it into poison. The net cast into the sea catches fish, not Bibles. The lost sheep in its absence from the flock is not transformed into a lion. The father is glad because of the prodigal's repentance, not displeased. Every particular of the parables is in full accordance with reality and law.

When flies hold converse with oxen—when asses array themselves in lions' skins—when foxes by invitation dine with cranes—when trees go forth to anoint a king—when deviations occur from Nature's steadfast laws—these things pertain to fables; or, to miracles, and not to parable. When Nathan narrated to King David his beautiful parable, it was accepted as actual history, so close was its resemblance to life. "As the Lord liveth the man that hath done this thing shall surely die," said the king. And this resemblance to reality was really necessary in order to accomplish the design of the parable—to draw from the king the verdict of "guilty," and to enable the prophet to speak those startling words, "Thou art the man."

The so-called parable of Jotham, in which events out of harmony with reason and law are narrated, is not a parable but a fable. Its design was not moral or religious instruction, but to set forth the folly of having Abimelech as king, while the design of the parable, and most certainly as used by Christ, is, to those able to understand it, always moral or religious instruction. But how a moral, for religious uses, can be drawn from events both imaginary and discordant with natural law, is certainly somewhat difficult to understand. Such events are contrary to the very nature of a parable. Every parable is a statement of something which resembles some other thing. And the interpretation always admits of being preceded by a "like," or "so" to indicate the resemblance. For instance, As a net cast into the sea, when full of fish, was drawn to shore; the fish were sorted; the good preserved, and the bad thrown away; so at the end of the world, shall angels sever the wicked from among the just, and cast them into the furnace of fire. Now the thing which the parable teaches, is affirmed to be like the thing which is stated in the parable; but it is impossible that the thing which the parable teaches can be like the thing which is stated in the parable if the latter be out of harmony with law; since the former is certainly in harmony with law. And by no possibility can what is out of harmony with law be like what is in harmony with law.

Whether the events narrated in a parable be imaginary or real is immaterial, but if imaginary they must necessarily, for the reason just given, be in harmony with reality and law—must be *like* what actually occurs. So far as the events of a parable are imaginary, so far of course it resembles in material a fable. But this clear distinction exists between the two. A fable admits into the material of its composition events discordant with reality and law; a parable, never. The events of a fable *may* be in harmony with realities; the events of a parable *must* be in such harmony.

With this idea of the nature of a parable, Trench in his "Notes on the Parables" coincides. He says, p. 12, remarking on the definition of a parable: " And yet again, there is another point of difference between the parable and the fable. While it can never be said that the fabulist is regardless of truth, since it is neither his intention to deceive, when he attributes language and discourse of reason to trees and birds and beasts, nor is any one deceived by him; yet the severer reverence for truth, which is habitual to the higher moral teacher, will not allow him to indulge, even in this sporting with the truth, this temporary suspension of its laws, though upon agreement, or at least with tacit understanding. In his mind, the creation of God, as it câme from the Creator's hands, is too perfect, has too much of reverence owing to it, to be represented otherwise than it really is. The great Teacher by parables, therefore, allowed himself in no transgression of the established laws of nature—in nothing marvelous or anomalous; he presents to us no speaking trees, or reasoning beasts, and we should be at once conscious of an unfitness in his doing so."

In addition to Trench, as confirming our idea of the nature of a parable, we cite the following authorities:

Strauss, the great rationalist of Germany, says in his Leben Jesu, vol. 1, p. 677, *seq.* (according to Trench, Notes on the Parables, p. 179): "While it is quite intelligible how the husbandmen should abuse and maltreat servants of their lord, who came demanding rent from them; it is inconceivable, and therefore could not find a place in a parable, of which the very condition is that it should have perfect verisimilitude—that invited guests, however unwilling to keep their engagement, should actually maltreat and kill the servants sent to remind them that the festival to which they were engaged, was ready." We are now concerned, not at all with the purpose of Strauss in asserting that " the very condition of a parable is that it should have '*perfect verisimilitude,*' " but merely with the assertion itself.

Fleming, as quoted in Worcester's unabridged dictionary, says: "The difference between a parable and an apologue is, that the former being drawn from human life, requires probability in the narration; whereas, the apologue being taken from inanimate things, or the inferior animals, is not confined strictly to probability. The fables of Æsop are apologues."

Webster's unabridged dictionary says: "An apologue differs from a parable in this: The parable is drawn from events which take place among mankind, and therefore requires probability in the narrative; the apologue is founded on supposed actions of brutes, or inanimate things, and therefore is not limited by strict rules of probability. Æsop's fables are good examples of apologues."

We may then, from the foregoing reasoning and testimony, legitimately conclude that no event of a parable of Christ can be out of harmony with either life or law.

And now before applying our conclusion permit us to refer once more to the testimony of the Missionary Thompson. On the parable of the great supper recorded in Luke xiv: and which is so peculiarly oriental and different from our. Western customs, he thus remarks: "If a shiekh, beg, or emir invites he always sends a servant to call you at the proper time. This servant often repeats the very formula mentioned in Luke xiv:17, *Tefuddulu el asha hader*—Come, for the supper is ready. The fact that this custom is mainly confined to the wealthy and to the nobility is in strict agreement with the parable, where the certain man who made the great supper, is supposed to be of this class.

It is true now as then that to refuse is a high insult to the maker of the feast, nor would such excuses as those in the parable be more acceptable to a Druse emir than they were to the Lord of this "great supper;" but, however angry, very few would manifest their displeasure by sending the servants into the highways and hedges after the poor, the maimed, the halt, the blind. All these characters are found in abundance in our streets, and I have known rich men who filled out the costume of the parable even in these particulars; it was, however, as matter of ostentation, to show the extent of their benevolence, and the depth of their humility and condescension. Nevertheless, it is pleasant to find enough of the drapery of this parable still practiced to show that originally it was, in all its details, in close conformity to the customs of this country." (Land and Book, Vol. I, pp. 178, 179.)

And now since Christ in the parable of the rich man and Lazarus, if it be a parable, represents a soul as, after physical death, suffering torment in Hades; and also that a fixed and impassable gulf prevents the suffering soul from passing over into bliss; and since no event of any parable of Christ is out of harmony with either life or law, therefore some souls after physical death do suffer torment in Hades, and a fixed and impassable gulf does prevent souls which suffer after physical death from passing over into bliss.

Thus it is seen that the passage taken as a parable bears the same testimony as when taken as a history; since the representations of the parable must be in accordance with fact. But, whether taken as a parable or a history it alike bears powerful testimony against the theory of final restoration. The lost soul suffers—the way of even a slight relief is blocked by a fixed and impassable gulf—and in response to supplication Abraham himself gives no single word of hope.

But here our Restorationist friends may remind us that, according to I Cor. xv:55, Hades is to be defeated; and may infer that in consequence of that defeat all sufferers in Hades will be freed from suffering. Hades will indeed be defeated, and could it be proved that subjection to the power of Hades is the sole cause of suffering beyond the grave, then the argument would be decisive that, on the defeat of Hades by all subject to its power, all suffering will cease. But since Christ after his physical death experienced no suffering; and yet after his physical death was subject to the power of Hades, therefore subjection to Hades is not the sole cause of suffering beyond the grave. And consequently release from Hades through its defeat does not terminate all cause of future suffering. And here it is proper to inquire as to the nature of the triumph over Hades which they are to gain who have been subject to its sway. Hades in I Cor. xv:55, as we have already ascertained (p. 119) means not the place of endless woe, but the world of the dead. As the world of the dead Hades is defeated and destroyed by a universal resurrection of the dead. But its total defeat by a universal resurrection furnishes no argument against endless perdition, unless the resurrection of the wicked dead necessitates their moral change from wickedness to holiness. But the Scriptures teach that neither in reference to the evil nor the good does the resurrection after physical death involve a change of moral character. Not in reference to Christ, for though he was raised with a holy character, yet he was holy when he died. Not in reference to those who sleep in Jesus, for they were believers when they died. Not in reference to the wicked dead, for Christ says in John v:28, 29, "All that are in the graves shall hear his voice and shall come forth; they that have done good unto the resurrection of life; and they that have done evil unto the resurrection of damnation." And none will affirm that they have holy characters who come forth into the resurrection of damnation. We freely admit that the resurrection of I Cor. xv. is a blessed resurrection; but in that resurrection the wicked dead have no part. It is confined to those who are accepted in Christ.

That resurrection of the wicked, therefore, which occurs after their physical death, leaves unchanged their moral character. In wickedness they die; in wickedness they are raised from death.

The total defeat of Hades, therefore, by a universal resurrection brings the wicked no nearer salvation than they were before.

And this fact furnishes an excellent reason why Abraham when supplicated by the soul suffering in Hades gave to the sufferer no words of hope. For, though sympathy may have invited, truthfulness would not allow.

Mark xiv:21: "The Son of man indeed goeth as it is written of him; but woe to that man by whom the Son of man is betrayed! good were it for that man if he had never been born." This statement of Jesus was made respecting an historical personage, and is, of course, to be regarded as true.

Yet on the theory of Restorationism, it can by no possibility be true. What living man would not endure the *restorative*, the *healing* sorrow of a day, inflicted under the eye of a loving God, for the joy of a lifetime?

Not one. If Judas ever escape from the

woe pronounced upon him, then the pain of that woe must possess a definite duration.

Should we call that duration a thousand years, then the *healing sorrow* of that thousand years would certainly be more than balanced by ten million years of joy. Should his restoration require ten thousand years, then the restorative pains of that ten thousand years would be more than balanced by a hundred million years of joy. We do not know that any Restorationist believes a longer time than ten thousand years will be required in the case of any sinner for the completion of the restorative process; but should it be thought to require even a thousand million of years, or the longest limited duration, even that long time would be far outbalanced by the strictly endless duration of happiness to follow. And therefore the truth of Jesus' words cannot be sustained on the theory of Restoration.

And since those words are true, therefore, the theory of restoration is false. But as any one may see, the words of Jesus are in perfect harmony with the belief that Judas is never to be restored from his doom.

Proposition VIII. Methods of interpretation which are used to make the Scriptures teach the final salvation of all, do also when applied to other passages, make the Scriptures teach the final condemnation of some (or all), but since these are contradictory doctrines, and since the Scriptures being revelations of a God of truth, do not teach contradictions, therefore, such methods of interpretation are wrong.

As instances of such wrong methods, we give the following:

1. Applying to mankind universally what is intended but for a portion of mankind.

Rev. xiii:14-17 is thus: "And deceiveth them that dwell on the earth by the means of these miracles which he had power to do in the sight of the beast; saying to them that dwell on the earth, that they should make an image to the beast which had the wound by a sword, and did live. And he had power to give life unto the image of the beast, that the image of the beast should both speak and cause that as many as would not worship the image of the beast, should be killed. And he causeth all, both small and great, rich and poor, free and bond, to receive a mark in their right hand or in their forehead. And that no man might buy or sell, save he that had the mark, or the name of the beast, or the number of his name."

Notice the apparent universality of the expression, "He causeth all, both small and great, rich and poor, free and bond, to receive a mark." Now, in the case of an advocate of universal restoration finding in the Scriptures a passage asserting the salvation of all as strongly as the above passage asserts, that all receive a mark, who is there that does not believe he would present that passage as a proof of universal salvation? Not one.

Yet notice now what is said in Rev. xiv: 9-11, of them who receive the mark: "And the third angel followed them, saying with a loud voice, 'If any man worship the beast and his image and receive his mark in his forehead or in his hand, the same shall drink of the wine of the wrath of God, which is poured out without mixture into the cup of his indignation; and he shall be tormented with fire and brimstone in the presence of the holy angels, and in the presence of the Lamb. And the smoke of their torment ascendeth up forever and ever; and they have no rest day or night who worship the beast and his image, and whosoever receiveth the mark of his name." Now this last passage clearly shows that all in the former passage did not mean all universally; but simply all without exception who were spoken of, and that they were many. And the same method of interpretation that teaches that the above passage or a similar one means all men universally, makes the Scriptures teach that all men universally are tormented with fire and brimstone in the presence of the holy angels and the Lamb; and that "the smoke of their torment ascendeth up forever and ever." This is certainly too bad for a world into which Christ has come.

2. Reasoning from God's creatorship, or from his Fatherhood through creatorship, or through covenant with special ones to universal salvation. Isa. lvii:16: "For I will not contend forever, neither will I be always wroth; for the spirits should fail before me, and the souls which I have made." Now if this passage means eternal salvation, it means the eternal salvation of the humble and contrite ones mentioned in the previous verse; not the eternal salvation of all men without exception. That it will not do to reason from the Creatorship of God or his Fatherhood through Creatorship to universal salvation, Isa. xxvii:11 clearly shows. "For it is a people of no understanding; therefore he that made them will not have

mercy on them, and he that formed them will show them no favor." If he will show them no favor they very certainly will never reach heaven. But since God made all men and says of all men, "There is none righteous, no not one ; there is none that understandeth," and since, being an impartial God, he will deal with them all upon the same principle, therefore he will show not one of them "favor," and then very certainly not one of them will ever reach heaven.

But this out-Herods Herod, and is certainly too bad for a world into which Christ has come, and in which he has a people who are "called and chosen and faithful."

3. Taking passages out of their proper connection and meaning.

God says, I John iii:15, " No murderer hath eternal life ;" but a murderer is one who has committed a murder ; therefore God says—no one who has committed a murder hath eternal life. And since God changes not, therefore He always says—no one who has committed a murder hath eternal life. And since God speaks truth, therefore no one who has ever committed a murder shall ever have eternal life. Of course by this wrong method of interpretation the Scriptures teach the final condemnation of some.

Now the final condemnation of some (or all), and the final restoration of all are contradictions; but since the Scriptures, being revelations of a God of truth, do not teach contradictions, therefore the above methods of interpretation which are used to make them so teach, are wrong. And since without using one or more of the above wrong methods of interpretation, it is impossible to make the Scriptures teach the doctrine of the final restoration of all, therefore, they do not teach that doctrine.

It is somewhat remarkable that the advocates of universal salvation combine all the above wrong methods in their interpretation of Isa. lvii:16.

They also tell us with one breath that the Old Testament does not reveal the doctrine of immortality, and with another breath that not only the doctrine of immortality, but also a blessed immortality for every child of Adam, is revealed in Isa. lvii:16. By some very convenient apparatus the same fountain flows hot and cold.

To further illustrate the folly of interpreting passages when they are isolated from their context, we quote from a journal the following sentence, "Its resistless momentum will annihilate us."* Get now, if you can, the idea which the writer means to convey by that sentence.

You doubtless think that he is referring to some fearful principle or power whose operation brings death or annihilation. And the certainty of annihilation is the idea which the sentence most naturally conveys. Yet the writer believes in, and is referring to "Universalism," and means by "us," those of his own faith.

Proposition IX. The teachings of Nature do not favor the idea that mankind universally will attain unto holiness and happiness.

John Ruskin, a man whose eminent intellectual abilities have the ear of the world, speaks as follows: "I understand not the most dangerous, because most attractive form of modern infidelity, which, pretending to exalt the beneficence of the Deity, degrades it into a reckless infinitude of mercy, and blind obliteration of the work of sin; and which does this chiefly by dwelling on the manifold appearances of God's kindness on

---

* Rev. E. W. Reynolds in "The Ambassador."

the face of creation. Such kindness is indeed everywhere and always visible, but not alone. Wrath and threatening are invariably mingled with the love; and in the utmost solitudes of nature, the existence of Hell seems to me as legibly declared by a thousand spiritual utterances as that of Heaven. It is well for us to dwell with thankfulness on the unfolding of the flower, and the falling of the dew, and the sleep of the green fields in the sunshine, but the blasted trunk, the barren rock, the moaning of the bleak winds, the roar of the black, perilous, merciless whirlpools of the mountain streams, the solemn solitudes of moors and seas, the continual fading of all beauty into darkness, and of all strength into dust; have these no language for us? We may seek to escape their teachings by reasonings touching the good which is brought out of all evil; but it is vain sophistry. The good succeeds to the evil as day succeeds the night, but so also the evil to the good. Gerizim and Ebal, birth and death, light and darkness, heaven and hell, divide the existence of man and his Futurity."

Rev. E. H. Chapin, D. D., a preacher of that Univeralism which believes in a limited punishment in the future life, speaks as follows: "Nature is not sufficient for us. We want to know what, if anything, exists behind nature, and works through nature. * * Sometimes in our thoughts there may arise the awful specter of a world without supervision, and without a controlling mind; a theater of unsubstantial forms, a domain of terrible and resistless forces, whose order is unguided by any sympathetic purpose, and in whose march we are trampled into annihilation. * * * Or if intellectual speculations do not stagger us, we may be troubled by moral doubts and fears. The evidences of divine goodness which are given us in the sunshine and the rain, may be counterbalanced by the instances of calamity and suffering which are so plentiful before our eyes. For not even the most genial nature—not one disposed to look upon the world with happiest eye, can deny the dark spots with which it is clouded; can deny that there are shades of mystery brooding over its deep places. And in conceiving of God, in trying to reach the conclusion that God is good, how many instances of perplexity, of seeming incongruity steal in to darken and overcloud our conviction and take away our faith in it. We look upon the earth, and it is as thickly strewn with the graves of the dead, as it is with the habitations of the living. It is teeming with instances of decrepitude and decay, as well as of life and development. And with all the rest, man, in any healthy state of his whole nature, in anything like a susceptible condition of his being, is conscious of sin. The universal consciousness is, that we are not wholly right within; that we have not walked perfectly and truly in the way that conscience dictates. And since that distinction between the right and the wrong, under a too frequent preponderance of the wrong in our acts, prevails within us, the thought sometimes springs up, that we may be separated from God—that God may be alienated from us. * * * If then, by our reason, we have attained the conception that there is a God—a God that cares for us—we have this feeling troubling us in that conception." * * * (Sermon on John iii:16, in The Ambassador). "I ask any man looking at the processes of sin—any thinking man who has ever looked beyond the surface of life; any man who has looked into his own heart, and felt the struggling forces contending there; any man who has ever felt the pressure of affliction bowing him to the earth—any man who knows the evil as well

as the good in his nature—I ask him if he does not want to know just this thing concerning the great God, that he loves him, and that he sent his only begotten Son into the world "that whosoever believeth in him should not perish but have everlasting life."
—*Ibid.*

Rev. I. D. Williamson, D. D., a preacher of that Universalism which believes in no punishment after death, speaks as follows: "The future is dark and gloomy to the mind that is not enlightened by the knowledge of Christ. The grave yawns in darkness at our feet, and what awaits us beyond that narrow house, no mortal man can tell."

R. W. Emerson, in an essay on Fate, speaks as follows: "Nature is no sentimentalist,—does not cosset or pamper us. We must see that the world is rough and surly, and will not mind drowning a man or woman; but swallows your ship like a grain of dust. The cold, inconsiderate of persons, tingles your blood, benumbs your feet, freezes a man like an apple. The diseases, the elements, fortune, gravity, lightning, respect no persons. The way of Providence is a little rude. The habit of snake and spider, the snap of the tiger and other leapers and bloody jumpers, the crackle of the bones of his prey in the coil of the anaconda,—these are in the system, and our habits are like theirs. You have just dined, and however scrupulously the slaughter house is concealed in the graceful distance of miles, there is complicity,—expensive races,—race living at the expense of race. The planet is liable to shocks from comets, perturbations from planets, rendings from earthquakes and volcano, alterations of climate, precessions of equinoxes. * * * At Lisbon an earthquake killed men like flies. At Naples, three years ago, ten thousand persons were crushed in a few minutes. The scurvy at sea; the sword of the climate in the west of Africa, at Cayenne, at Panama, at New Orleans, cut off men like a massacre. Our Western prairie shakes with fever and ague. The cholera, the smallpox have proved as mortal to some tribes as a frost to the crickets, which, having filled the summer with noise, are silenced by a fall of the temperature of one night. Without uncovering what does not concern us, * * * the forms of the shark, the *labrus*, the jaw of the sea-wolf paved with crushing teeth, the weapons of the grampus, and other warriors hidden in the sea,—are hints of ferocity in the interiors of nature. Let us not deny it up and down. Providence has a wild, rough, incalculable road to its end, and it is of no use to try to whitewash its huge, mixed instrumentalities, or to dress up that terrific benefactor in a clean shirt and white neckcloth of a student of divinity. Will you say the disasters which threaten mankind are exceptional, and one need not lay his account for cataclysms every day? Aye, but what happens once, may happen again, and so long as these strokes are not to be parried by us, they must be feared."

We now go back of the Christian era and give the testimony of two most eminent heathen philosophers.

Plato in his Phædon represents Socrates as thus discoursing shortly before his death : "My friends, there is still one thing which it is very just to believe, and this is, that if the soul be immortal, it requires to be cultivated with attention, not only for what we call the time of life, but for that which is to follow— I mean eternity ; and the least neglect in this point may be attended with endless consequences. If death were the final dissolution of being, the wicked would be great gainers by it, as being delivered at once from their bodies, their souls, and their vices; but as the soul is immortal, it has no other means of being freed from its evils, nor any safety for itself, but in becoming very good and very prudent; for it carries nothing away with it but its good or bad deeds, its virtues or vices, which are commonly the consequence of the education it has received, and the causes of eternal happiness or misery. When the dead are arrived at the fatal rendezvous of departed souls whither their dæmon conducts them, they are all judged. * * * Those who are judged to be incurable on account of the greatness of their crimes, who deliberately and wilfully have committed sacrileges and murders, and other such great offences, the fatal destiny that passes judgment upon them, hurls them into Tartarus, from whence they never depart."

In his Republic I. V., Plato speaks thus: " When one supposes himself near the point of death, there enter into his soul fear and anxieties respecting things before unheeded. For then the old traditions concerning Hades, how those who in this life have been guilty of wrong, must there suffer the penalty of their crimes, torment his soul. He looks back upon his past life, and if he finds in the record many sins, like one starting from a frightful dream he is terrified, and filled with foreboding fears."

Let us now notice some testimonies given in their last hours by certain wicked men.

Voltaire the infidel exclaims, "I am abandoned by God and man." "Doctor, I will give you half of what I am worth if you will give me six months' life." And on the doctor's replying, " Sir, you cannot live six weeks," said, "Then I shall go to hell."

Francis Spira exclaimed : "Who can succor a soul oppressed by a sense of sin, and by the wrath of God? It is Jesus Christ alone who must be the physician, and the gospel is the only antidote." "My sin is greater than the mercy of God. I have denied Christ voluntarily, and against my convictions. I feel that he hardens me and will allow me no hope." "It is a fearful thing to fall into the hands of the living God." " I feel the weight of his wrath burning like the pains of hell within me, and pressing on my conscience with an anguish which cannot be described."

Charles IX, King of France, who sanctioned the massacre of St. Bartholomew, by which perhaps 50,000 people were murdered in cold blood, said in anguish on the death bed, "Ah, my nurse, my dear nurse, what blood, what murders! Oh, what evil counsels I have followed! Oh my God, pardon me, and have mercy on me if thou canst. I know not what I am. What shall I do? I am lost. I see it well."

Francis Newport, infidel, in his last hours said: "Would you be informed why I am become a skeleton in three or four days? See then how I have despised my Maker and denied my Redeemer; I have joined myself to the atheists and profane, and continued this course under many convictions, till my iniquity was ripe for vengeance, and the just judgment of God overtook me when my security was the greatest, and the checks of my conscience were the least. How idle is it to bid the fire not burn when fuel is administered, and to command the seas to be smooth in the midst of a storm! Such is my case." To an inquiry of a friend as to his condition he replied, "Lost forever." He continued, "Ah, the forlorn hopes of him that has not God to go to! Nothing to fly to for peace or comfort. God is become my enemy, and there is none so strong as to deliver me out of his hands. He consigns me over to eternal vengeance, and there is none able to redeem me! Were there such another God as he who would patronize my cause; or were I above God, or independent of him; could I act or dispose of myself as I pleased; then would my horrors cease, and the expectations and designs of my formidable enemies be frustrated. But oh, this cannot be, for I— Oh, the insufferable pangs of hell and damnation."

One whom Dr. Young names Altamont, in his last hours said thus: "Remorse for the past throws my thoughts on the future; worse dread of the future strikes them back on the past. I turn and turn, and find no ray. Didst thou feel half the mountain that is on me, thou wouldst struggle with the martyr for his stake, and bless heaven for the flame; that is not an everlasting flame— that is not an unquenchable fire." "My principles have poisoned my friend; my extravagance has beggared my boy; my unkindness has murdered my wife! And is there another hell? Oh! thou blasphemed, yet most indulgent Lord God! Hell itself is a refuge, if it hide me from thy frown."

Here we have Orthodox, Universalist and infidel alike testifying that nature does not teach that mankind universally will attain to final happiness.

Here we have philosophic heathen affirming that endless retribution awaits, beyond the grave, the extremely wicked; and that the wicked, when thinking themselves near death, are terrified and filled with foreboding fears. Here we have the wicked in their dying hours believing and exclaiming that they are going to an endless hell. Where shall we find better interpreters of nature? If those who believe in Revelation be suspected of prejudice, what shall be said of the infidel, the heathen, and the dying?

So far is nature from teaching a blessed immortality to every child of Adam that she teaches no immortality at all. She does through certain mental powers and natural facts point to a future life, but whether that life is unending or not, no mortal ear ever heard nature tell.

The utmost that nature teaches on the subject of human happiness is, that so long as man is continued in existence and lives in harmony with certain of nature's laws, happiness results from that harmony; and that so long as man is continued in existence and lives out of harmony with certain of nature's laws, pain results from that lack of harmony. Nature has no heart. She gives pain just as readily as she gives pleasure. She says, In this way of life be happy—in that way of life be wretched—take your choice. Nature is just as impartial as the Universalist's God. She will drown a babe of days as quick as a pirate. She will roast a pious missionary as quick as a dark skinned cannibal. She will pinch with hunger a St. Paul as quick as a Nero. She will kill a president Lincoln as quick as a Wilkes Booth. And does such a mistress teach a universal and immortal happiness?

Nay, she teaches just as Revelation teaches, that a certain amount of infraction of laws designed for happiness brings death—death forever.

A finger, an ear, a head cut off, nature never restores. Life destroyed by poison or bullet she never rebuilds. Occasionally in India she starves some half a million of human beings to death, not one of them has she ever brought back to life. Through the long generations she has fertilized the earth with dead human bones; when has she clothed them with flesh and beauty?

When nature is seen to inflict none but a beneficial pang to the individual; when seas refuse to drown shipwrecked sailors; when flames of fire refuse to scorch innocent children; when laws of gravitation refuse to dash into pieces on the lower rocks the unfortunate who has fallen from the precipice; when the now deadly poison refuses to act on the physical frame of the would be suicide; when nature rectifies all human errors and heals all human woes, then, and not till then, assert that she teaches the final happiness of universal man.

Proposition X. Endless punishment, though it be a fact, does not prove that God is unjust.

The following statements of Universalists show their views on the punishment of sin: "The punishment of sin is swift, sure and inevitable." "So far from destroying the fear of retribution, Universalism quickens it, by showing that the punishment of sin cannot be avoided." (Mr. Whittemore, Plain Guide, pp. 262, 263.) "No man can by any possibility escape the just punishment of his sins." (Mr. Williamson, Exposition of Universalism, p. 65.) "Justice will have all its demands; every man shall suffer to the full extent of his deserts. There is no remission of sin, either on account of the Saviour's death, or the sinner's penitence." (Mr. Skinner, Univ. Illus., p. 249.) "It [the Bible] never teaches the forgiveness or remission of punishment for sins committed. It is the forgiveness of *sins;* by which is, understood, the blotting out, or cleansing from, after due justice is administered." (Mr. Fernald, Univ. against Partialism, p. 259.) "The person who has been forgiven has suffered the proper punishment of his sins." (Mr. Skinner, Univ. Illus. and Defen., p. 252.) "We are the only denomination who believe that *all sin* will be punished." (Mr. Williamson, Exp. of Univ., p. 15.)

The above statements imply or assert the following: 1. That man is a sinner.

2. That God has punished, does punish, or will punish each individual sinner personally to the full extent of his deserts.

3. That though God has thus punished sinners on earth from the time of Adam's first sin until now, and will thus punish sinners on earth from now until the resurrection hour, yet he is still a just God.

Now, since every sinner must receive his full desert of punishment, it necessarily follows that such sinners as do not receive their full desert of punishment in this life, must receive some punishment in the next life. From this conclusion there is no escape. The inquiry now arises, Do all sinners without exception receive their full desert of punishment in this life?

1. Let us notice some instances in which

sinners were taken out of this life while they were still wicked.

The inhabitants of Sodom were sinners of this class. At the time of Abraham's petition for the guilty city there were not ten righteous within it. And no one will claim that, after the petition and before the destruction, all the inhabitants ceased from all wickedness.

But if not then at the moment of their destruction the inhabitants were committing sin. Now, should the opposers of future punishment affirm that physical death is a full punishment of all sin, it would in this case be an untrue affirmation.

For the physical destruction of the Sodomites was determined upon because of sins before the prayer of Abraham. And consequently the full punishment of their last sin could not be that same physical death. And the question now arises, Do the Scriptures teach that the punishment of a special act of sin terminates at the time in which that special act terminates? And unless the affirmative of this question can be shown, punishment continues after death. Now, the Scriptures in every single instance in which the punishment of sin is referred to, teach us that the punishment does not terminate with the act of sin, but continues sharp and severe long after that act terminates. Cain exclaiming that his punishment is greater than he can bear; Jacob's exile and suffering in consequence of his act of deception; the brethren of Joseph saying one to another, long years after their crime, "We are verily guilty concerning our brother;" the punishments of Adam and Achan; of Haman and Jezebel; of the Jewish nation and of everyday life, all teach us that the punishment of sin does not terminate with the act of sin. But if it be affirmed that all the punishment which God designs to inflict upon the sinner, does terminate with the special act of sin, then, in accordance with that design, throw open the doors of your prisons; call off your detectives from the track of the robber and the murderer; erase from your law books every penalty for crime; abolish every national agreement for the suppression of piracy; lift not a finger for the suppression of rebellion; for why shall mere man punish him whom God has already punished to the full?

But since punishment for sin does not terminate with the act of sin, therefore, the punishment of the last sins of the Sodomites reached or will reach into the life which is subsequent to physical death. And since this punishment which reaches the Sodomites subsequent to their physical death is just, therefore God is just in inflicting it.

The same mode of reasoning will apply to the antediluvians perishing in the deluge; to every wicked man killed in his wickedness; and to every impenitent man dying under the sentence of the Almighty.

Thus the very doctrine which disbelievers in future punishment have by unnatural interpretations wrenched out of the Scriptures—the doctrine that no sinner can escape his full desert of punishment even though he truly repent, and truly believe in Jesus Christ—the doctrine which was designed to explode, and which they assert does explode the doctrine of Christ's atonement, does itself explode their own system. They are "hoist with their own petard."

That our conclusion is correct concerning the punishment of the Sodomites in the future state, the Saviour teaches in a passage before referred to: "It shall be more tolerable for Sodom and Gomorrah in the day of judgment than for that city."

2. We now notice certain persons who have departed this life by their own hands.

The public journals lately stated that a criminal arrested in the city of New York attempted first to shoot the arresting officer, but failing through the snapping of the cap, placed the muzzle of the pistol in his own mouth and killed himself. Now since no one will affirm that every criminal who takes his own life is so exceedingly crazy as to be entirely free from responsibility, we will take for granted that there was responsibility in the case of this criminal. Placed in a painful position by his own fault, he commits an additional crime by attempting to kill an innocent officer, and then a further crime by killing himself. Now should we even admit that conscience and detection had sufficiently punished him for the crime for which he was arrested, what shall be said of the attempt to kill the officer; and of the actual killing of himself? Those who deny that punishment is inflicted in the future state, also deny that repentance and faith in Christ can free the transgressor from the slightest penalty of his transgression. They affirm that the sinner must suffer in his own person, the full penalty of his sin.

Now in what possible way did this criminal receive before death the full penalty of both his attempt to kill, and his actual self-killing?

The whole affair was momentary, and if the full punishment of the attempt to kill, and the self-killing was experienced in the short space of time between the snapping of the cap and his own death, then there is no escape from the conclusion that God has attached but a very slight penalty for such crimes. Why, a good and conscientious little child will suffer more from a decayed tooth, or from disobedience to some parental command, than that murderer and suicide suffered between his attempt to kill and his death.

Now let us make the supposition that the cause of this criminal's arrest was actual murder; that for months he had succeeded in escaping arrest; that at the time of his arrest he actually murdered the policeman; that in this last murder he contracted guilt as great as in the first, and that immediately after killing the policeman he killed himself. Now, in this supposed case, while the guilt of the two murders is equal, and of necessary consequence the penalty also equal, the penalty suffered for the first murder is far greater than the penalty suffered for the second murder. The one may have been endured five months, the other not five seconds. In this case what makes up the full penalty of the second murder? Not the pains of physical death. These Paul and even Jesus experienced. Not death itself; this the best of men do not escape. Not the speediness of death; for, according to the deniers of future punishment, the more speedy the death the more speedily terminates all penalty and all suffering. Nothing makes it up; and if their affirmation that no sinner can escape the full penalty of his sin, be true, then, by necessary consequence, it follows that sinners like this sinner suffer or will suffer just punishment in the life subsequent to physical death.

The cases of Ahithophel and Judas Iscariot are quite similar. Both committed a crime and soon afterward died by their own hands. And the statement of the Saviour respecting the latter, "It had been good for that man if he had not been born," confirms the conclusion which we have reached, that some sin is justly punished in the life beyond the grave. Now wherever to a finite being there comes punishment for sin, there, apart from God's promise to the contrary, it is perfectly reasonable to conclude that additional sin may be committed. Now God has in the Scriptures given no promise that a person dying in impenitence shall not commit sin in the future life.

And further, a person thus dying, and in the future life receiving just punishment, must love God with all his heart—must be perfectly holy, or he cannot but sin. For this love and this holiness God always commands. And anything less than a perfect obedience to the command of God is sin. But if the man died unreconciled to God, what, between the moment of his death and the moment of his punishment in the future state, made him perfectly holy? No promise of this perfect holiness is given to such an one in the Scriptures. Does the mere fact of physical death impart to them this perfect holiness? There is no reason to believe it. And there are passages in the Scriptures which oppose it. The sin unto death for which we are not commanded to pray: The sin against the Holy Ghost which shall be forgiven neither in this world nor in the world to come. The resurrection unto damnation, which under a previous proposition we have showed that Christ taught: The belief of the martyred son and saint that Antiochus would have no resurrection unto life: The assertion of Paul that at Christ's second coming the wicked shall be punished with everlasting destruction from the presence of the Lord and the glory of his power—these make the doctrine anti-scriptural. But being anti-scriptural, it is untrue. Therefore when in the next life the punishment begins, the one punished is unholy. But every moral being during every moment of unholiness is committing additional sin. And every additional sin deserves additional punishment. And thus apart from the regenerating power of God, it will continue forever. Now since we have no authority in nature or Scripture for believing that God will in the next life regenerate—make holy those sinners who in the earthly life reject Jesus Christ and the Holy Spirit; since there is a sin unto death;—since the end of some sinners is according to their works; since the end of some sinners is destruction; since at Christ's second coming some sinners will be punished with everlasting destruction from the presence of the Lord and the glory of his power, therefore God may never regenerate those who in the next life are unholy. But if God never regenerate them they will sin as long as they live. Therefore God may punish them as long as they live, and still be just. They may live forever, therefore God may punish them forever and still be just.

We add a series of questions and answers on somewhat kindred topics. The answers are thought to be such as either reason or the principles of his own belief will necessitate a Restorationist to give.

ON THE LOVE OF GOD.

1. Is the love of God for moral agents originated and regulated by their moral worth, or by the principles of his own nature? Ans. By the latter.

2. Will the principles in the nature of God which originate and regulate his love for moral agents ever change? Ans. No.

3. Since the principles of the nature of God which regulate his love for moral agents will never change, have we any reason whatever, apart from revelation, for believing that moral agents will be dealt with any more favorably at any future time than they are now? Ans. No.

4. Does not the God of infinite love now allow his moral creatures to commit sin and incur punishment in consequence of the commission of sin? Ans. Yes.

5. Since the God of infinite love does now allow his moral creatures to commit sin and incur consequent punishment, should the time ever arrive when he does not allow his moral creatures to sin and incur consequent punishment, will he not deal more favorably with his moral creatures then than now? Ans. Yes.

6. Since, revelation apart, we have no reason for believing that God will at any

time deal more favorably with his moral creatures than now; and since should the time come when it can be truthfully said, "He does not allow his moral creatures to sin and incur consequent punishment," he will deal more favorably with them then, than now, have we, apart from revelation, any reason for believing that such time will ever arrive? Ans. No.

7. Since apart from revelation, we have no reason for believing that such time will ever arrive, have we any reason apart from revelation for believing that sin and consequent suffering will ever cease? Ans. No.

ON THE ATTRIBUTES OF GOD.

1. Does God always, without exception, act in harmony with his attributes? Ans. Yes.

2. Do any of God's moral creatures sin against him? Ans. Yes.

3. Is God's suffering moral creatures to sin against him in harmony with his attributes? Ans. Yes.

4. Is God a being of infinite perfection? Ans. Yes.

5. If God changes not, must not that which is in harmony with his attributes now, be in harmony with his attributes always? Ans. Yes.

6. Will God change? Ans. No.

7. Since the infinitely perfect God changes not, and since his suffering moral creatures to sin against him is in harmony with his attributes *now;* for how long a duration must his suffering moral creatures to sin against him be in harmony with his attributes? Ans. Forever.

ON THE BEST RESULT.

1. As a creature of God does man, through his whole existence, receive what God deems best, or what man deems best? Ans. What God deems best.

2. Does what God deems best always agree with what man deems best? Ans. No.

3. Can, then, what man deems best be a rule to decide what God deems best? Ans. No.

4. If then, man deems it best that all mankind be brought to final holiness and happiness, does man's deeming it best prove that God deems it best? Ans. No.

5. Since man receives through his whole existence not what he deems best, but what God deems best; and since man's deeming final universal holiness and happiness best is no proof that God so deems, is man's deeming final universal holiness and happi-

ness best, any proof of final universal holiness and happiness? Ans. No.

ON THE DIVINE ELECTION.

1. Does God design that all men shall believe in Christ in the temporal life? Ans. No.

2. Does God design that some men shall believe in Christ in the temporal life? Ans. Yes.

3. Which is the happier in this life, the believer or the unbeliever? Ans. The believer.

4. Which enters eternity in the more desirable condition, the believer or the unbeliever? Ans. The believer.

5. Does not the believer then have the advantage both in this life and in eternity, over the unbeliever? Ans. Yes.

6. Who caused that the believer has an advantage both in this life and in eternity, over the unbeliever? Ans. God.

7. Could not God have caused all men in this life to have equal faith in Christ, and to enter eternity under circumstances of equal desirableness? Ans. Yes.

8. Does not God then deal more favorably in this life and the next, with some men than with others? Ans. Yes.

9. Since God does deal, both in this life and the next, more favorably with some men than with others, is not such dealing perfectly consistent with all God's attributes? Ans. Yes.

10. Since God is perfect and unchangeable, is not his dealing more favorably with some men than with others forever, perfectly consistent with all God's attributes? Ans. Yes.

11. Is not God's dealing more favorably with some men than with others forever the very principle of the doctrine of divine election? Ans. Yes.

12. Since God's dealing more favorably forever with some men than with others is perfectly consistent with all his attributes; and since God's dealing more favorably forever with some men than with others is the very principle of the doctrine of the divine election, is not the very principle of the doctrine of divine election perfectly consistent with all God's attributes? Ans. Yes.

13. Is not that principle reasonable which is perfectly consistent with all God's attributes? Ans. Yes.

14. Is not he who denies the reasonableness of a principle which is perfectly

consistent with all God's attributes himself unreasonable? Ans. Yes.

15. Since he who denies the reasonableness of a principle which is perfectly consistent with all God's attributes, is himself unreasonable; and since the principle of the doctrine of the divine election is perfectly consistent with all God's attributes, is not he who denies the reasonableness of the principle of the doctrine of the divine election himself unreasonable? Ans. Yes.

And now, as humanity stands amid a thousand dangers, there comes to listening ears a *voice* saying, "*I am the good Shepherd; I am the resurrection and the life; before Abraham was, I am; I am he that liveth, and was dead; and behold I am alive forever more. Come unto me all ye that labor and are heavy laden and I will give you rest.*" Through the grace of Almighty God may it be the happy experience of every reader of this little book to hear and heed that loving voice.

<blockquote>
Swinging to and fro, to and fro,
  The pendulum doth go,
And soon the day is gone.
Swinging to and fro, to and fro,
  The day and night doth go,
And soon this life is done.
</blockquote>

www.ingramcontent.com/pod-product-compliance
Lightning Source LLC
Chambersburg PA
CBHW031332230426
43670CB00006B/324